TEACHING JOHNNY TO THINK

A Philosophy of Education Based on the Principles of Ayn Rand's Objectivism

LECTURES BY **LEONARD PEIKOFF**

EDITED BY **MARLENE TROLLOPE**

AYN RAND INSTITUTE PRESS

PREFACE

People have often asked for a written version of my oral lecture courses, on the premise—with which I agree—that written lectures are much more accessible to the student. Writing, however, is in this context virtually a different language from speaking; a raw transcript of an extemporaneous speech, however excellent, is almost always filled with defects and confusions of one sort or another—and so is frequently boring as well. To turn a lecture course into an accurate, clear, and valuable book, a huge amount of time-consuming editing is required, a task which can be performed only by an individual with the necessary motivation, knowledge of the subject, and editorial skills. My own age and priorities make it impossible for me to undertake such a task.

I have therefore decided to authorize several individuals who possess the necessary qualifications to edit and bring out in book form certain of my courses, and to do so entirely without my participation. Although I have confidence in these editors to the extent that I know them, I have had no part in their work at any stage—no guiding discussions, no reading of transcripts, not even a glance at early drafts or final copy. Even a glance might reveal errors, and I could not then evade the need to read more, and so forth, which is precisely what is out of the question.

The only exception to the above is the article on American education written and edited by me in 1984. This article, which can serve as a generalized preface to the book, is placed immediately after this statement.

In my opinion, the lecture course presented in this book is of real value to those interested in the subject. But when you read it, please bear two things in mind: Marlene Trollope is an experienced editor and teacher—and I have no idea what she has done in this book.

P.S. If you happen to spot and wish to point out seeming errors in the text, please email Marlene Trollope at the Ayn Rand Institute c/o mail@ aynrand.org. If you like this book, I may add, do not give me too much of the credit. My course provided, let us say, the spirit, but Marlene Trollope gave it the flesh required to live.

Leonard Peikoff
April 10, 2012

The American School:
Why Johnny Can't Think*

We are now a few hours from Income Tax Day in George Orwell's year—an ominous moment, symbolically, when we feel acutely the weight of an ever growing government, and must begin to wonder what will happen next and how long our liberty can last.

The answer depends on the youth of the country and on the institutions that educate them. The best indicator of our government tomorrow is our schools today. Are our youngsters being brought up to be free, independent, thinking men and women? Or are they being turned into helpless, mindless pawns, who will run into the arms of the first dictator that sounds plausible?

One does not have to be an Objectivist to be alarmed about the state of today's schools. Virtually everybody is in a panic over them—shocked by continually falling SAT scores; by college entrants unable to write, spell, paragraph, or reason; by a generation of schoolteachers so bad that even teachers-union president Albert Shanker says of them: "For the most part, you are getting illiterate, incompetent people who cannot go into any other field."[1]

Last November a new academic achievement test was given to some six hundred sixth-grade students in eight industrialized countries. The American students, chosen to be representative of the nation, finished dead last in mathematics, miles behind the Japanese, and sixth out of eight in science. As to geography, 20 percent of the Americans at one school could not find the United States on a world map. The *Chicago Tribune* reported these findings under the headline: "Study hands world dunce cap to U.S. pupils."[2]

A year ago, the National Commission on Excellence in Education described the United States as "a nation at risk," pointing to what it called "a rising tide of mediocrity [in our schools] that threatens our very future

---

* Note: This lecture was delivered at the Ford Hall Forum on April 15, 1984, and published in *The Objectivist Forum*, October–December 1984.

1. Quoted in *USA Today*, August 12, 1983.

2. December 12, 1983.

as a nation and as a people."[3] These are extreme words for normally bland government commissioners, but the words are no exaggeration.

To prepare for this evening's discussion, I did some first-hand research. I spent two weeks in February visiting schools in New York City, both public and private, from kindergarten through teachers college. I deliberately chose schools with good reputations—some of which are the shining models for the rest of the country—and I let the principals guide me to their top teachers. I wanted to see the system not when it was just scraping by, starved for money and full of compromises, but at its best, when it was adequately funded, competently staffed, and proud of its activities. I got an eyeful.

My experience at one school, a famous Progressive institution, will serve to introduce my impression of the whole system. I had said that I was interested in observing how children are taught concepts, and the school obligingly directed me to three classes. The first, for nine- and ten-year-olds, was a group discussion of thirteen steps in seal-hunting, from cutting the hole in the ice at the start to sharing the blubber with others at the end. The teacher gave no indication of the purpose of this topic, but he did indicate that the class would later perform a play on seal-hunting and perhaps even computerize the steps. The next class, for thirteen-year-olds, consisted of a mock Washington hearing on the question of whether there should be an import tax on Japanese cars. Students played senators, Japanese lobbyists, Lee Iacocca, and so on, and did it quite well; the teacher sat silently, observing. I never learned the name of this course or of the seal-hunting one, but finally I was to observe a meeting described to me as a class in English. At last, I thought, an academic subject. But no. The book being covered was Robert Kennedy's *Thirteen Days*, a memoir of the Cuban missile crisis of 1962. A typical topic for discussion was whether a surgical air strike against Cuba would have been better policy than a blockade.

The school, undoubtedly, would defend these classes as exercises in ethnicity or democracy or relevance, but, whatever the defense, the fact is that all these classes were utterly concrete-bound. Seal-hunting was not used to illustrate the rigors of northern life or the method of analyzing a skill into steps or *anything* at all. The issue of taxing Japanese cars was not related to a study of free trade vs. protectionism, or of the proper function of government, or of the principles of foreign policy, or of any principles. The same applies to the Cuban discussion. In all cases,

---

3. Quoted in *New York Times*, April 27, 1983.

a narrow concrete was taught, enacted, discussed, argued over in and of itself, that is, as a concrete, without connection to any wider issue. This is the essence of the approach that, in various forms, is destroying all of our schools: the *anti-conceptual* approach.

Let me elaborate for a moment on the crucial philosophic point involved here.

Man's knowledge begins on the perceptual level, with the use of the five senses. This much we share with the animals. But what makes us human is what our mind does with our sense experiences. What makes us human is the *conceptual* level, which includes our capacity to abstract, to grasp common denominators, to classify, to organize our perceptual field. The conceptual level is based on the perceptual, but there are profound differences between the two—in other words, between perceiving and *thinking*. Here are some of the differences; this is not an exhaustive list, merely enough to indicate the contrast.

The perceptual level is concerned only with concretes. For example, a man goes for a casual stroll on the beach—let's make it a drunken stroll so as to numb the higher faculties and isolate the animal element—and he sees a number of concrete entities: those birds chattering over there, this wave crashing to shore, that boulder rolling downhill. He observes, moves on, sees a bit more, forgets the earlier. On the conceptual level, however, we function very differently; we integrate concretes by means of abstractions, and thereby immensely expand the amount of material we can deal with. The animal or drunk merely looks at a few birds, then forgets them; a functioning man can retain an unlimited number, by integrating them all into the *concept* "bird," and can then proceed deliberately to study the nature of birds, their anatomy, habits, and so forth.

The drunk on his walk is aware of a vast multiplicity of things. He lurches past a chaos made of waves, rocks, and countless other entities, and has no ability to make connections among them. On the conceptual level, however, we do not accept such chaos; we turn a multiplicity into a *unity* by finding the common denominators that run through all the seemingly disconnected concretes, and we thereby make them intelligible. We discover the law of gravity, for example, and grasp that by means of a single principle we can understand the falling boulder, the rising tide, and many other phenomena.

On the perceptual level, no special order is necessary. The drunk can totter from bird to rock to tree in any order he wishes and still see them all. But we cannot do that conceptually; in the realm of thought, a definite progression is required. Since we build knowledge on previous knowledge, we need to know the necessary background, or context, at each stage. For example, we cannot start calculus before we know arithmetic—or argue about tariff protection before we know the nature of government.

Finally, for this brief sketch: on the perceptual level, there is no need of logic, argument, proof; a man sees what he sees, the facts are self-evident, and no further cognitive process is required. But on the conceptual level, we do need proof. We need a method of validating our ideas; we need a guide to let us know what conclusions follow from what data. That guide is logic.

Perception as such, the sheer animal capacity, consists merely in staring at concretes, at a multiplicity of them, in no order, with no context, no proof, no understanding—and all one can know by this means is whatever he is staring at, as long as he is staring. Conception, however—the distinctively human faculty—involves the formation of abstractions that reduce the multiplicity to an intelligible unity. This process requires a definite order, a specific context at each stage, and the methodical use of logic.

Now let us apply the above to the subject of our schools. An education that trains a child's mind would be one that teaches him to make connections, to generalize, to understand the wider issues and principles involved in any topic. It would achieve this feat by presenting the material to him in a calculated, conceptually proper order, with the necessary context, and with the proof that validates each stage. This would be an education that teaches a child to think.

The complete opposite—the most perverse aberration imaginable—is *to take conceptual-level material and present it to the students by the method of perception.* This means taking the students through history, literature, science, and the other subjects on the exact model of that casual, unthinking, drunken walk on the beach. The effect is to exile the student to a no-man's-land of cognition, which is neither perception nor conception. What it is, in fact, is destruction, the destruction of the minds of the students and of their motivation to learn.

This is literally what our schools are doing today. Let me illustrate by indicating how various subjects are taught, in the best schools, by the best teachers. You can then judge for yourself why Johnny can't think.

I went to an eighth-grade class on Western European history in a highly regarded, non-Progressive school with a university affiliation. The subject that day was: Why does human history constantly change? This is an excellent question, which really belongs to the philosophy of history. What factors, the teacher was asking, move history and explain men's past actions? Here are the answers he listed on the board: competition among classes for land, money, power, or trade routes; disasters and catastrophes (such as wars and plagues); the personality of leaders; innovations, technology, new discoveries (potatoes and coffee were included here); and developments in the rest of the world, which interacts with a given region. At this point, time ran out. But think of what else could qualify as causes in this kind of approach. What about an era's press or media of communication? Is that a factor in history? What about people's psychology, including their sexual proclivities? What about their art or their geography? What about the weather?

Do you see the hodgepodge the students are being given? History, they are told, is moved by power struggles and diseases and potatoes and wars and chance personalities. Who can make sense out of such a chaos? Here is a random multiplicity thrown at a youngster without any attempt to conceptualize it—to reduce it to an intelligible unity, to trace the operation of principles. This is perceptual-level history, history as nothing but a torrent of unrelated, disintegrated concretes.

The American Revolution, to take a specific example, was once taught in the schools on the conceptual level. The Revolution's manifold aspects were identified, then united and explained by a principle: the commitment of the colonists to individual rights and their consequent resolve to throw off the tyrant's yoke. This was a lesson students could understand and find relevant in today's world. But now the same event is ascribed to a whole list of alleged causes. The students are given ten (or fifty) causes of the Revolution, including the big landowners' desire to preserve their estates, the Southern planters' desire for a cancellation of their English debts, the Bostonians' opposition to tea taxes, the Western land speculators' need to expand past the Appalachians, and so forth. No one can retain such a list longer than is required to pass the exam; it must be memorized, then regurgitated, then happily and thoroughly forgotten. That is all one can do with unrelated concretes.

If the students were taught by avowed Marxists—if they were told that history reflects the clash between the factors of production and the modes of ownership—it would be dead wrong, but it would still be a principle, an integrating generalization, and it would be much less harmful to the students' ability to think; they might still be open to argument on the subject. But to teach them an unconceptualized hash is to imply that history is a tale told by an idiot, without wider meaning, or relevance to the present. This approach destroys the possibility of the students thinking or caring at all about the field.

I cannot resist adding that the State Education Department of New York has found a way, believe it or not, to make the teaching of history still worse. You might think that, in history at least, the necessary *order* of presenting the material is self-evident. Since each era grows out of the preceding, the obvious way to teach events is as they happened, that is, chronologically. But not according to a new proposal. In order "to put greater emphasis on sociological, political, and economic issues," a New York State proposal recommends that historical material be organized for the students according to six master topics picked out of the blue from the pop ethos: "ecology, human needs, human rights, cultural interaction, the global system of economic interdependence, and the future." In this approach, an event from a later period can easily be taught (in connection with one master topic) first, long before the developments from an earlier period that actually led to it. As a more traditional professor from Columbia has noted: "The whole thing would be wildly out of chronological order. The [Russian] purge trials of the 1930s would be taught before the revolutions of 1905 and 1917. It is all fragmented and there is no way that this curriculum relates one part of a historical period to another, which is what you want kids to be able to do."[4] But the modern educators don't seem to care about that. They *want* "fragments," that is, concretes, without context, logic, or any other demands of a conceptual progression.

I do not know what became of this New York proposal. The fact that it was announced to the press and discussed seriously is revealing enough.

Given the way history is now being taught, it is not surprising that huge chunks of it promptly get forgotten by the students or simply are never taken in. The result is many adolescents' shocking ignorance of the most elementary historical, or current, facts. One man wrote a column recently in *The Washington Post* recounting his conversations with today's teenagers. He found high school graduates who did not know anything about World War II, including what happened at Pearl Harbor, or what country the United States was fighting in the Pacific. "Who won?" one college student asked him. At one point, the writer and a girl who was a junior at the University of Southern California were watching television coverage of Poland after martial law had been imposed; the set showed political prisoners being put into a cage. The girl could not understand it.

"'Why don't they just leave and come to L.A.?'" she asked.

---

4. *New York Times*, April 18, 1983; the professor is Hazel Hertzberg.

"I explained that they were not allowed to leave."

"'They're not?'" she said. "'Why not?'"

"I explained that in totalitarian states citizens usually could not emigrate."

"'They can't?'" she said. "'Since when? Is that something new?'"[5]

Now let us make a big jump—from history to *reading*. Let us look at the method of teaching reading that is used by most American schools in some form: the look-say method (as against phonics).

The method of phonics, the old-fashioned approach, first teaches a child the sound of individual letters; then it teaches him to read words by combining these sounds. Each letter thus represents an abstraction subsuming countless instances. Once a child knows that *p* sounds "puh," for instance, that becomes a principle; he grasps that every *p* he meets sounds the same way. When he has learned a few dozen such abstractions, he has acquired the knowledge necessary to decipher virtually any new word he encounters. Thus the gigantic multiplicity of the English vocabulary is reduced to a handful of symbols. This is the conceptual method of learning to read.

Modern educators object to it. Phonics, they say (among many such charges), is unreal. I quote from one such mentality: "There is little value in pronouncing the letter *p* in isolation; it is almost impossible to do this—a vowel of some sort almost inevitably follows the pronunciation of any consonant."[6] This means: when you pronounce the sound of *p*—"puh"—you have to utter the vowel sound "uh"; so you haven't isolated the pure consonant; so phonics is artificial. But why can't you isolate *in your mind*, focusing only on the consonant sound, ignoring the accompanying vowel for purposes of analysis—just as men focus on a red table's color but ignore its shape in order to reach the concept "red"? Why does this writer rule out selective attention and analysis, which are the very essence of human cognition? Because these involve an act of abstraction; they represent a conceptual process, precisely the process that modern educators oppose.

Their favored method, look-say, dispenses with abstractions. Look-say forces a child to learn the sounds of whole words without knowing the sounds of the individual letters or syllables. This makes every word a new concrete to be grasped only by perceptual means, such as trying to remember its distinctive shape on the page, or some special picture the

5. Benjamin J. Stein, "The Cheerful Ignorance of the Young in L.A.," October 3, 1983.

6. Pose Lamb, *Linguistics in Proper Perspective*, 2nd ed. (Charles E. Merrill: 1977), p. 29.

teacher has associated with it. Which amounts to heaping on the student a vast multiplicity of concretes and saying: stare at these and memorize them. (You may not be surprised to discover that this method was invented, as far as I can tell, by an eighteenth-century German professor who was a follower of Rousseau, the passionate opponent of reason.)

There is a colossal Big Lie involved in the look-say propaganda. Its advocates crusade *against* the overuse of memory; they decry phonics because, they say, it requires a boring memorization of all the sounds of the alphabet. Their solution is to replace such brief, simple memorization with the task of memorizing the sound of every word in the language. In fact, if one wishes to save children from the drudgery of endless memorization, only the teaching of abstractions will do it—in any field.

No one can learn to read by the look-say method. It is too anti-human. Our schools today, therefore, are busy teaching a new skill: guessing. They offer the children some memorized shapes and pictures to start, throw in a little phonics (thanks to immense parental pressure), count on the parents secretly teaching their children something at home about reading—and then, given this stew of haphazard clues, they concentrate their efforts on teaching the children assorted methods of guessing what a given word might be.

Here is a look-say expert describing a child's proper mental processes when trying to determine the last word of the sentence, "They make belts out of plastic." The child must not, of course, try to sound out the letters. Here is what should go on in his brain instead:

"Well, it isn't leather, because that begins with l. My mother has a straw belt, but it isn't straw either. It looks like a root. I'll divide it between *s* and *t*. There couldn't be more than two syllables because there are only two vowels. Let's see—*p, l, a, s*. One vowel and it's not at the end of the syllable . . ." This goes on a while longer, and the child finally comes up with: "Oh, sure, plastic! I'm surprised I didn't think of that right away because so many things are made of plastic." The expert comments: "Just described is a child who was not about to carry out a letter-by-letter analysis of *plastic* if it wasn't necessary, which is exactly right."[7]

Can you imagine reading *War and Peace* by this method? You would die of old age before you reached the third chapter.

I must add that the look-say educators demand that children—I quote another devotee—"receive praise for a good guess even though it is not

---

7. Dolores Durkin, *Strategies for Identifying Words*, p. 83; quoted in Rudolf Flesch, *Why Johnny* Still *Can't Read* (Harper Colophon: 1983), p. 81.

completely accurate. For example, if a child reads 'I like to eat carrots' as 'I like to eat cake,' praise should be given for supplying a word that makes sense and follows at least some of the phonic cues."[8]

How would you like to see, at the head of our army, a general with this kind of schooling? He receives a telegram from the president during a crisis ordering him to "reject nuclear option," proceeds to make a good guess, and reads it as "release nuclear option." Linguistically, the two are as close as "carrots" and "cake."

The result of the look-say method is a widespread "reading neurosis" among children, a flat inability to read, which never existed in the days of phonics (and also a bizarre inability to spell). In 1975, for example, 35 percent of fourth-graders, 37 percent of eighth-graders, and 23 percent of twelfth-graders could not read simple printed instructions. The U.S. literacy rate, it has been estimated, is now about equal to that of Burma or Albania, and by all signs is still dropping. Do you see why angry parents are suing school systems for a new crime: educational malpractice?

Now let us look at another aspect of English studies: the teaching of *grammar*. This subject brings out even more clearly the modern educators' contempt for concepts.

Grammar is the study of how to combine words—that is, concepts—into sentences. The basic rules of grammar—such as the need of subject and predicate, or the relation of nouns and verbs—are inherent in the nature of concepts and apply to every language; they define the principles necessary to use concepts intelligibly. Grammar, therefore, is an indispensable subject; it is a science based entirely on facts—and not a very difficult science, either.

Our leading educators, however, see no relation between concepts and facts. The reason they present material from subjects such as history without conceptualizing it is precisely that they regard concepts as mental constructs without relation to reality. Concepts, they hold, are not a device of cognition, but a mere human convention, a ritual unrelated to knowledge or reality, to be performed according to arbitrary social fiat. It follows that grammar is a set of pointless rules, decreed by society for no objectively defensible reason.

I quote from a book on linguistics written for English teachers by a modern professor: "Because we know that language is arbitrary and changing, a teacher's attitude toward nonstandard usage should be one

---

8. Dixie Lee Spiegel, in *The Reading Teacher*, April 1978; quoted in Flesch, *Why Johnny* Still *Can't Read*, p. 24.

of acceptance. . . . One level of language is not 'better' than another; this is why the term *nonstandard* is preferable to *substandard* in describing such usage as 'He don't do it,' 'Was you there?' A person who uses terms such as these will probably be penalized in terms of social and educational advancement in our society, however, and it is for this reason that the teacher helps children work toward, and eventually achieve, standard usage, perhaps as a 'second' language."[9] In short, there is no "correct" or "incorrect" any more, not in any aspect of language; there is only the senseless prejudice of society.

I saw the results of this approach in the classroom. I watched an excellent public-school teacher trying to explain the possessive forms of nouns. She gave a clear statement of the rules, with striking examples and frequent repetition; she was dynamic, she was colorful, she was teaching her heart out. But it was futile. This teacher was not a philosopher of language, and she could not combat the idea, implicit in the textbook and in all the years of the students' earlier schooling, that grammar is purposeless. The students seemed to be impervious to instruction and incapable of attention, even when the teacher would blow a shrieking police whistle to shock them momentarily into silence. To them, the subject was nothing but senseless rules: the apostrophe goes here in this case, there in that one. Here was a whole science reduced to disintegrated concretes that had to be blindly memorized—just like the ten causes of the American Revolution, or the ten shapes of the last look-say session.

You might wonder how one teaches *composition*—the methods of expressing one's thoughts clearly and eloquently in writing—given today's philosophy of grammar and of concepts. I will answer by reading excerpts from a recent manifesto.

"We affirm the students' right to their own patterns and varieties of language—the dialects of their nurture or whatever dialects in which they find their own identity and style. . . . The claim that any one dialect is unacceptable amounts to an attempt of one social group to exert its dominance over another." If so, why does anyone need English teachers?

Who issued this manifesto? Was it some ignorant, hotheaded teenagers drunk on the notion of student power? No. It was the National Council of Teachers of English.[10]

If you want a hint as to the basic philosophy operative here, I will

---

9. Lamb, *Linguistics in Proper Perspective*, p. 19.
10. From "Students' Right to Their Own Language," Conference on College Composition and Communication, Fall 1974; quoted in Arn and Charlene Tibbetts, *What's Happening to American English?* (New York: Scribner's, 1978), p. 118.

mention that the editor of *College English*, one of the major journals of the profession, objects to "an industrial society [that] will continue to want from us—or someone else—composition, verbal manners, discipline in problem solving, and docile rationality."[11] Note how explicit this is. The climax of *his* "enemies list" is "rationality."

Despite today's subjectivism, some rules of composition are still being taught. Certain of these are valid enough, having been carried over from a better past. But some are horrifying. Here is an exercise in how to write topic sentences. The students are given two possible sentences with which to start a paragraph, then are asked to choose which would make a good opening and which a bad one. Here is one such pair:

1. Cooking is my favorite hobby.

2. It really isn't hard to stir-fry Chinese vegetables.

The correct answer? Number 1 is bad. It is too abstract. (!) Students should not write about so enormous a subject as an entire hobby. They should focus only on one concrete under it, such as Chinese vegetables.

Here is another pair:

1. There is too much pollution in the world.

2. We have begun to fight pollution in our own neighborhood.

Of course, number 1 is inadmissible. Students must not think about world problems—that is too vague—only about the dinky concretes in their own backyard.[12]

This sort of exercise has been consciously designed to *teach* students to be concrete-bound. How are children with such an upbringing ever to deal with or think about problems that transcend Chinese vegetables and their own neighborhood? The implicit answer, absorbed by the students unavoidably, is: "You don't have to worry about things like that; society or the president will take care of you; all you have to do is adapt."

Before we leave English, I want to mention what has been happening to the teaching of *literature* in our schools as a consequence of the

---

11. See *College English*, February 1976, p. 631; quoted in Tibbetts, *What's Happening*, p. 119.

12. Joy Littell, *Practice Book: Basic Skills in English*/Orange Level (McDougal, Littell), p. 17.

attitude toward concepts that we have been discussing. First, there has been the disappearance from the schools of the classics in favor of cheap current novels. The language and themes of the classics are too difficult for today's students to grasp; one does not teach Shakespeare to savages, or to civilized children being turned into savages. Then, there is the continuous decline even of today's debased standards. I quote from two English teachers: "Years ago we used to hear that *Julius Caesar* was too difficult for ninth-graders; now we are told that *Lord of the Flies* is too hard for the general run of tenth-graders." Then, there is the final result, now increasingly common: the disappearance of literature of any kind and its replacement by what are called "media classes." These are classes, in one book's apt description, that "teach television, newspapers, car-repair magazines, and movies."[13]

I will pass up all the obvious comments on this frightening descent. I have just one question about it: Why should these graduates of TV and car-repair magazines care if the great books of the past are burned by government edict—when they can't read them anyway?

Turning to the teaching of *science* in our schools, I want to mention an instructive book written by two professors at Purdue University; titled *Creative Sciencing*, it tells science teachers how to teach their subject properly. To learn science, the book declares, students must engage in "hands-on science activities." They must perform a series of concrete "experiments," such as designing a bug catcher, collecting pictures of objects that begin with a *c*, going on field trips to the local factory, or finding polluters in the community. (These examples are taken from the book.) There is no necessary order to these activities. The children are encouraged to interact with the classroom materials "in their own way," as the mood strikes them. They are not to be inhibited by a teacher-imposed structure or by the logic of the subject.[14]

You may wonder whether students taught in this manner will ever learn the abstract concepts and principles of science, the natural laws and explanatory theories that have been painstakingly discovered across the centuries—the knowledge that makes us civilized men rather than jungle primitives.

The answer has been given by F. James Rutherford, chief education officer of the American Association for the Advancement of Science. "We're too serious," he declared. "We insist on all the abstract stuff. We

13. Tibbetts, *What's Happening*, pp. 80, 76.

14. Alfred DeVito and Gerald H. Krockover, *Creative Sciencing* (Little, Brown: 1980), pp. 15, 70, 74.

need to relax and let the children learn their own neighborhood." This statement was made at a meeting of experts brought together by a large foundation to discover what ails science teaching.[15]

Today's education, I have said, reduces children to the status of animals, without the ability to know or predict the future. Animals, however, can rely on brute instinct to guide them. Children cannot; brought up this way, they soon begin to feel helpless—to feel that everything is changing and that they can count on nothing.

The above is not merely my polemic. The science teachers are working deliberately to create this state of mind. The teachers are openly skeptical themselves, having been given a similar upbringing, and they insist to their students that everything is changing, that factual information is continually becoming outdated, and that there are things much more important in class—in *science* class—than truth. It is hard to believe how brazen these people have become. "When preparing performance objectives," the *Creative Sciencing* book says, "you may wish to consider the fact that we don't demand accuracy in art or creative writing, but we have permitted ourselves to require accuracy in science. We may be paying a high price in lost interest, enthusiasm, vitality, and creativity in science because of this requirement of accuracy."[16]

Our students should not have to be concerned about factual accuracy. They need have no idea whether gases expand or contract under pressure, or whether typhus germs cause or cure disease—but this will leave them free to be "vital" and "creative."

But, you may ask, what if a student comes out in class with a wrong answer to a factual question? You are old-fashioned. There is no such answer, and besides it would be bad for the student's psychology if there were: "How many times will a student try to respond to a question if continually told that his or her answers are wrong? Wrong answers should be reserved for quiz shows on television."[17]

What then is the point in having a teacher at all?—since there are no wrong answers, and since adults must not be "authoritarian," and since, as John Dewey has proclaimed, students do not learn by listening or by reading, but only by "doing." This brings me to an extremely important issue, one that is much wider than science teaching.

My overriding impression of today's schools, derived from every

---

15. Quoted in *New York Times*, January 31, 1984.

16. DeVito and Krockover, *Creative Sciencing*, p. 33.

17. Ibid., p. 38.

class I visited, is that teachers no longer teach. They no longer deliver prepared material while the students listen attentively and take notes. Instead, what one encounters everywhere is *group-talking*, that is, class participation and class discussion. Most of the teachers I saw were enthusiastic professionals, excellent at what they do. But they conceive their role primarily as bull-session moderators. Some of the teachers obviously had a concealed lesson in mind, which they were bootlegging to the students—in the guise of asking leading questions or making brief, purposeful side comments. But the point is that the lesson had to be boot-legged. The official purpose of the class was for the pupils to speak more or less continually—at any rate, well over half the time.

I asked one group of high school students if their teachers ever deliv-ered *lectures* in class. "Oh no!" they cried incredulously, as though I had come from another planet or a barbaric past. "No one does that anymore."

All the arguments offered to defend this anti-teaching approach are senseless.

"Students," I have heard it said, "should develop initiative; they should discover knowledge on their own, not be spoon-fed by the teach-ers." Then why should they go to school at all? Schooling is a process in which an expert is paid to impart his superior knowledge to ignorant beginners. How can this involve shelving the expert and leaving the ignorant to shift for themselves? What would you think of a doctor who told a patient to cure himself because the doctor opposed spoon-feeding?

"Students," I have heard, "should be creative, not merely passive and receptive." How can they be creative before they know anything? Creativity does not arise in a void; it can develop only *after* one has mastered the current cognitive context. A creative ignoramus is a con-tradiction in terms.

"We teach the method of thought," I have heard, "rather than the content." This is the most senseless claim of all. Let us leave aside the obvious fact that method cannot exist apart from some content. The more important point here is that *thought* is precisely what cannot be taught by the discussion approach. If you want to teach thought, you must first put up a sign at the front of the class: "Children should he seen and not heard." To be exact: they may be heard as an adjunct of the lesson, if the teacher wishes to probe their knowledge, or answer a question of clarifi-cation, or assess their motivation to learn, or entertain a brief comment. But the dominant presence and voice must be that of the teacher, the cog-nitive expert, who should be feeding the material to the class in a highly purposeful fashion, carefully balancing concretes and abstractions, preparing for and then drawing and then interrelating generalizations, identifying the evidence at each point, and so forth. These are the processes that must first be absorbed year after year by the student in relation to a whole series of different contents. In the end, such training will jell in his mind into a knowledge of how to think—which he can then apply on his own, without any teacher. But he can never even begin to grasp these processes in the chaotic hullabaloo of a perpetual class discussion with equally ignorant peers.

Have you seen the [1984] television debates among the Democrats seeking to be president? Do you regard these spectacles of arbitrary assertion, constant subject-switching, absurd concrete-boundedness, and brazen *ad hominem* as examples of thinking? This is exactly the pattern that is being inculcated as thinking today by the class-discussion method.

An educator with any inkling of the requirements of a conceptual consciousness would never dream of running a school this way. But an educator contemptuous of concepts, and therefore of knowledge, would see no objection to it.

In the class discussions I saw, the students were regularly asked to state their own opinion. They were asked it in regard to issues about which they had no idea *how* to have an opinion, since they had no knowledge of the relevant facts or principles, and no knowledge of the methods of logical argument. Most of the time the students were honest; they had no opinion, in the sense of a sincere, even if mistaken, conviction on the question at hand. But they knew that they were expected to "express themselves." Time and again, therefore, I heard the following: "I like (or dislike) X." "Why?" "Because I do. That's my opinion." Whereupon the teacher would nod and say "very interesting" or "good point." Everybody's point, it seemed, was good, as good as everybody else's, and reasons were simply irrelevant. The conclusion being fostered in the minds of the class was: "It's all arbitrary; anything goes and no one really knows." The result is not only the spread of subjectivism, but of a self-righteous subjectivism, which cannot even imagine what objectivity would consist of.

Project a dozen years of this daily processing. One study of American students notes that they "generally offered superficial comments . . . and consultants observed that they seemed 'genuinely puzzled at requests to explain or defend their points of view.'"[18] What else could anyone expect?

Now let me quote from a *New York Times* news story.

---

18. "Are Your Kids Learning to Think?" *Changing Times*, December 1983; quoting the National Assessment of Educational Progress.

"I like [Senator Gary Hart's] ideas," said Darla Doyle, a
Tampa homemaker. "He's a good man. His ideas are fresher
than Mondale's are. I like the way he comes across."

A reporter asked Mrs. Doyle to identify the ideas that
appealed to her. "That's an unfair question," she said, asking
for a moment to consider her answer. Then she replied, "He
wants to talk with Russia."

The headline of this story is: "Hart's Fans Can't Say Why They Are."[19]

According to John Dewey, students are bored by lectures, but motivated to learn by collective "doing." Not the ones I saw. Virtually every
class was in continuous turmoil, created by students waving their hands
to speak, dropping books, giggling, calling out remarks, whispering
asides, yawning, fidgeting, shifting, shuffling. The dominant emotion
was a painful boredom, which is the sign of minds being mercilessly
starved and stunted. Perhaps this explains the magic influence of the bell.
The instant it rang, everywhere I went, the room was empty, as though
helpless victims were running for their lives from a dread plague. And
so in a sense they were.

Our schools are failing in every subject and on a fundamental level.
They are failing methodically, as a matter of philosophic principle. The
anti-conceptual epistemology that grips them comes from John Dewey
and from all his fellow irrationalists, who dominate twentieth-centu-
ry American culture, such as linguistic analysts, psychoanalysts and
neo-Existentialists. And behind all these, as I argued in *The Ominous
Parallels*, stands a century of German philosophy inaugurated by history's greatest villain: Immanuel Kant, the first man to dedicate his life and
his system to the destruction of reason.

Epistemological corruption is not the only cause of today's educational fiasco. There are many other contributing factors, such as the
teachers unions, and the senseless requirements of the teachers colleges,
and the government bureaucracies (local and federal). But epistemology
is the *basic* cause, without reference to which none of the others can be
intelligently analyzed or remedied.

Now let me recount for you two last experiences, which bear on the
political implications of today's educational trend.

One occurred at the most prestigious teacher-training institution in
the country, Teachers College of Columbia University.

---

19. March 9, 1984.

In my first class there, chosen at random, the professor made the following pronouncement to a group of sixty future teachers: "The evil of the West is not primarily its economic exploitation of the Third World, but its ideological exploitation. The crime of the West was to impose upon the communal culture of Africa the concept of the individual." I thought I had heard everything, but this shocked me. I looked around. The future teachers were dutifully taking it down; there were no objections.

Despite their talk about "self-expression," today's educators have to inculcate collectivism. Man's organ of individuality is his mind; deprived of it, he is nothing, and can do nothing but huddle in a group as his only hope of survival.

The second experience occurred in a class of juniors and seniors at a high school for the academically gifted. The students had just returned from a visit to the United Nations, where they had met with an official of the Russian delegation, and they were eager to discuss their reactions. The class obviously disliked the Russian, feeling that his answers to their questions about life in Russia had been evasions or lies. But soon someone remarked that we Americans are accustomed to believing what our government says, while the Russians naturally believe theirs. "So how do I know?" he concluded. "Maybe everything is a lie."

"What is truth?" asked one boy, seemingly quite sincere; the class laughed, as though this were obviously unanswerable.

"Neither side is good," said another student. "Both countries lie all the time. But the issue is the percentage. What we need to know is how much they lie—is it 99 percent for one, for example, and 82 percent for the other?"

After a lot more of this, including some pretty weak arguments in favor of America by a small patriotic faction, one boy summed up the emerging consensus. "We can never know who is lying or telling the truth," he said. "The only thing we can know is bare fact. For example, we can know that a Korean airliner was shot down by the Russians [in 1983]. But as to the Russians' story of the cause vs. our story, that is mere opinion."

To which one girl replied in all seriousness: "But we can't even know that—none of us saw the plane shot down."

This class discussion was the climax of my tour. I felt as though I were witnessing the condensed essence of a perceptual-level schooling. "Thought," these students were saying, "is helpless, principles are non-existent, truth is unknowable, and there is, therefore, no way to choose between the United States of America and the bloodiest dictatorship in history, not unless we have seen the blood with our own eyes."

These youngsters represent the future of our country. They are the children of the best and the brightest, who will become the businessmen, the artists, and the political leaders of tomorrow. Does this kind of generation have the strength—the intellectual strength, the strength of conviction—necessary to uphold the American heritage in an era dominated by incipient Big Brothers at home and missile-rattling enemies abroad?

It is not the students' fault, and they do not fully believe the awful things they say, not yet. The ones I saw, at every school except for Columbia—and here I want to register some positive impressions—were extremely likable. For the most part, they struck me as clean-cut, well-mannered, exuberant, intelligent, innocent. They were not like the typical college student one meets, who is already hardening into a brash cynic or skeptic. These youngsters, despite all their doubts and scars, still seemed eager to discover some answers, albeit sporadically. They were still clinging to vestiges of the idea that man's mind can understand reality and make sense of the world.

They are still open to reason—if someone would teach it to them.

Nor is it basically the teachers' fault. The ones I saw were not like the college professors I know, who reek of stale malice and delight in wrecking their students' minds. The teachers seemed to take their jobs seriously; they genuinely liked their classes and wanted to educate them. But given the direction of their own training, they were unable to do it.

There is a whole generation of children who still want to learn, and a profession much of which wants to help them, to say nothing of a country that devoutly wishes both groups well. Everything anyone would need to save the world is there, it is waiting, and all that is required to activate it is . . . what?

Merit pay? First we need a definition of merit, that is, of the purpose of teaching. More classes in the use of computers? We have enough children who know FORTRAN but not English. Compulsory community service? (A recommendation of the Carnegie Commission.) Prayer in the schools? (President Reagan's idea of a solution.)

All these are the equivalent of sticking Band-Aids on (or in the last two cases knives into) a dying man. The only real solution, which is a precondition of any other reform, is a philosophic change in our culture. We need a philosophy that will teach our colleges—and thereby our schoolteachers, and thus finally our youngsters—an abiding respect, a respect for reason, for man's mind, for the conceptual level of consciousness. That is why I subscribe to the philosophy of Ayn Rand. Hers is the only such philosophy in America today. It could be the wonder cure that would revive a generation.

The National Committee on Excellence in Education declared, "If an unfriendly foreign power had attempted to impose on America the mediocre educational performance that exists today, we might well have viewed it as an act of war."[20] Intellectually speaking, however, we *are* under the yoke of a foreign power. We are under the yoke of Kant, Hegel, Marx, and all their disciples. What we need now is another Declaration of Independence—not political independence from England this time, but philosophical independence from Germany.

To achieve it would be a monumental job, which would take many decades. As part of the job, I want to recommend one specific step to improve our schools: close down the teachers colleges.

There is no rational purpose to these institutions (and so they do little but disseminate poisonous ideas). Teaching is not a skill acquired through years of classes; it is not improved by the study of "psychology" or "methodology" or any of the rest of the stuff the schools of education offer. Teaching requires only the obvious: motivation, common sense, experience, a few good books or courses on technique, and, above all, a knowledge of the material being taught. Teachers must be masters of their subject; this—not a degree in education—is what school boards should demand as a condition of employment.

This one change would dramatically improve the schools. If experts in subject matter were setting the terms in the classroom, some significant content would have to reach the students, even given today's dominant philosophy. In addition, the basket cases who know only the Newspeak of their education professors would be out of a job, which would be another big improvement.

This reform, of course, would be resisted to the end by today's educational establishment, and could hardly be achieved nationally without a philosophic change in the country. But it gives us a starting point to rally around that pertains specifically to the field of education. If you are a parent or a teacher or merely a concerned taxpayer, you can start the battle for quality in education by demanding loudly—even in today's corrupt climate—that the teachers your school employs know what they are talking about, and then talk about it.

"If a nation expects to be ignorant and free . . . ," wrote Thomas Jefferson, "it expects what never was and never will be."[21]

---

20. Quoted in *New York Times*, April 27, 1983.
21. *The Jeffersonian Cyclopedia*, "Freedom and Education," p. 274.

Let us fight to make our schools once again bastions of *knowledge*. Then no dictator can rise among us by counting, like Big Brother in *1984*, on the enshrinement of ignorance.

And then we may once again have a human future ahead of us.

TEACHING JOHNNY TO THINK

A Philosophy of Education Based on the
Principles of Ayn Rand's Objectivism

CONTENTS

INTRODUCTION

Leonard Peikoff is the foremost authority on the ideas of Ayn Rand and her philosophy, Objectivism. He has delivered countless lectures and written numerous articles; teaching, clarifying and expounding the principles of this philosophy. He is the author of *The Ominous Parallels: The End of Freedom in America* and *Objectivism: The Philosophy of Ayn Rand*, the manifestation of her total philosophy in one place. His most recent book is *The DIM Hypothesis: Why the Lights of the West Are Going Out.*

In his article "Why Johnny Can't Think," Dr. Peikoff asked the question, "Are our children being educated to be free, independent, thinking men and women?" The obvious response led him to develop a reality-based, fully integrated model for the proper training of a rational mind. Applying Objectivist epistemology and ethics to the field of education, his 1985 lecture series, Philosophy of Education, was the result—a systematic, conceptual approach for "teaching Johnny to think." It serves as an antidote for the anti-conceptual approach he witnessed during his research in American schools. It articulates the methods, curriculum, and structure that develop the cognitive tools children require to deal successfully with the world—and dramatically demonstrates how an educational system's philosophical base impacts every fiber of that organization.

My goal was to faithfully transcribe into print the content of the course, revising for repetitions, self-corrections, grammar, and the occasional quotation for which no source could be found. Additionally, certain segues were required in print that were self-evident orally. I also wanted to preserve as much as possible the nuances and emphases conveyed by the human voice in a live presentation. This was especially important because Dr. Peikoff was demonstrating in his presentation the very methods he was lecturing on; practicing what he was preaching, in essence. Just as a translation from French to English may not possess the full flavor of the original, so with speech to text. However, every effort was made to retain the integrity of his delivery, his conversational tone, and teaching style.

I chose to incorporate Dr. Peikoff's responses to questions following the lectures directly into the main body of the text where applicable. These were often clarifications of points, additional examples or related information not addressed in the lecture, such as his view on Montessori education. This lent a greater coherence to the material as opposed to including the Q&A sessions separately at the end of each chapter.

It is both a personal pleasure and, as a teacher, a welcome educational obligation to offer this tremendous value to a reading audience. *Teaching Johnny to Think* is for parents and teachers struggling to educate today's youth—those who are keen to teach something sound and meaningful that is missing from current bloated and ineffectual school systems—something that speaks to the need for rigor and excellence—something that brings the entire world into a child's mental grasp.

But additionally, anyone who hopes to communicate effectively or to persuade others, anyone who values independent thought and seeks to foster it in themselves and others, can benefit from the material that Dr. Peikoff presents.

On a broader perspective, *Teaching Johnny to Think* supplies ammunition and a proper, rational alternative for those concerned individuals honestly striving to remedy our schools through social and political means.

Those within the forever-burgeoning educational bureaucracy seek to accommodate all comers, capitulating to every new pressure group, the perpetually offended politically correct set, and similar vested interests. The disastrous results are apparent to anyone. And schools move further and further away from their prime purpose—to prepare youth to face, with independence and confidence, the challenges of leading a productive and fulfilling life in the real world.

The need to implement Dr. Peikoff's philosophy of education with its clear goals, proper cognitive methodology, rational structure, and rigorous curriculum could not be more critically urgent.

Marlene Trollope

September 2012

CHAPTER ONE

The Nature and Purpose of Education

The criticism of education, its declining standards and ill-prepared students has had many voices, including mine. Yet very little of a positive nature in the overall field of "what should education be?" has been done. *Teaching Johnny to Think* endeavors to provide an answer.

The first task in any serious undertaking is to define the terms. In order to fully understand the concepts developed and to approach them from a mutual context, we must share a noncontroversial, philosophically neutral, general definition of education that will orient us to the field. This definition is basically obtained by raiding several good dictionaries: Education is *systematic* instruction of *the young* to develop in them *the powers* necessary for *mature life*.

The word *systematic* indicates that to qualify as education, a process must be deliberate, organized, and long range. It is a process of years that takes place in steps or stages aimed at a definite result. Education is not the haphazard, short-range accumulation of snippets of data. If you let a child loose in the jungle, he would undoubtedly learn a fair amount of information, the way wolf-boys do, but it would be scattered, disorganized concretes. That is not education. Education is a long-term, organized process. The term *systematic* stresses the distinction between a specific concrete skill or item of information on the one hand and education in general, on the other.

In that sense, it is a parallel to science. Many people can learn isolated scientific facts, but it is only science when you have a systematic knowledge acquired through reason, as differentiated from random pieces of data. The point here is any major human endeavor has to be organized, purposeful, and systematic if it is to achieve its goals. Education is an essential of human life. In that sense, it is contrasted to the need of animals. Birds get tips from their parents, but they get them briefly, in no special order, and then they are thrown out of the nest to fend for themselves. They do not have an education, as we are here defining it.

Education is a distinctively human need. Do not confuse "education" with "schooling." It is possible to be educated at home and some authorities even think this is preferable. Education does not necessarily include "learning from others." Such a phenomenon is called an autodidact, a self-educated individual. In these extraordinarily rare cases, a person typically gets some teaching from others, and then finishes the job himself, but that also comes within our concept of "education." Our focus is on the broad essence of education, wherever it is given, whether by parents, teachers, or in part by yourself—and that is systematic instruction.

Why "*of the young*"? Adult education is typically remedial. In other words, some adults never learned as youngsters what they needed. They are trying to acquire what is really a need of their youth. Thus, it still reflects the general idea that education is a need of the young. Adults may also learn a specialized skill or a specialized body of knowledge. For instance, if you want to go on a trip to Spain, you may learn Spanish, and that is commonly called "education." Similarly, becoming a proficient typist is not an education, although it may be part of one. This is not education in the basic sense that we are concerned with. It is training in a concrete skill. You could say that it is a continuation of the educational process that preceded it. Education can go on all your life because you can go on learning. But for our purposes, *education* is those skills and knowledge that you need to function as an adult.

Education is concerned with developing the general powers of the child. Consider the distinction between ethics and etiquette. An etiquette course gives you concretes, such as how to hold a fork and knife. It has a very circumscribed application to particular social behaviors such as dining. An ethics course gives you advice and principles on how to live your entire life in every situation. It is concerned with the fundamentals that shape your whole existence. Education, in that sense, is a parallel to ethics, not to etiquette. When we devote ten or twenty years to schooling, the purpose is to bring out general abilities and aptitudes for all of life. The purpose is to transform the child into a different being; to develop new capacities and powers that he did not have before.

The idea of education is to take a *tabula rasa* (someone born blank) and transform him, through a systematic process across years, into a being with the skills and aptitudes necessary to fit him for adult life. This raises many questions. What kind of systematic instruction and in what? What powers are to be developed? What powers are necessary to mature life, and by what means can they be imparted? What is mature life? What kind of demands does it make on us?

You see at once how philosophy enters the picture here because all of these questions can be answered only by reference to a philosophy. In particular, for the philosophy of education, you need two critical subjects: *epistemology* and *ethics*.

Epistemology is the study of how the mind operates, how it learns, how man—including the child—knows. That is the absolute precondition for any discussion of how to train the mind or how to impart new knowledge to it. You may hold that reason is man's only means of knowledge or you may hold that faith is the essential means of knowledge. Those two different theories of epistemology will have the most radical effects on your theory of education: how and what to communicate to a child. The same is true if you hold that man can acquire certainty or you hold that he cannot. That is purely an epistemological question, but it will redound throughout every aspect of education.

Ethics dictates the answers to such questions as: What does mature life consist of? Do we want to prepare the child for social adaptation, self-expression, or something else? What is important and worthwhile in life? What does the child have to learn, to aim at, to appreciate, to cope with, and what is dispensable, insignificant, or positively harmful?

A philosophy of education is the application of epistemology and ethics to issues of education. The whole field can be approached only from a philosophic basis, and once you have that viewpoint, it is much easier to determine what to do in education.

With that brief orientation, I do need to say a word to motivate you to read this book. (Chapter 2 will make clear why I think it is important to do so.) The primary beneficiaries of a book on the philosophy of education are parents and teachers, those concerned directly with children. If you are a teacher, it should be obvious why this book is of value to you. This is your life work, training children in something. It is assumed that you want to know in what and for what purpose. If a teacher is anything other than the lowest hack, it is essential that he or she have this knowledge. If you are a parent, this material is crucial because parents are the ones responsible for their child's maturation. You cannot just accept what the teacher says, particularly today. You have to know: Are they equipping my child properly or are they harming him? Are they giving him the essentials he needs to develop properly? What are the essentials? If he is having trouble in school, is that his problem or is that the fault of the school? What are the schools doing, and is that what they should be doing? A philosophy of education, in short, is essential to being a proper parent; otherwise, you are merely turning your child over to blind chance. Even if you happen to have good teachers, you have to supplement their work at home in order to enhance your child's ability to succeed.

There are two other groups that I think can benefit. First, anybody who wants to communicate, teach, or persuade others of specific things—a husband and a wife, an employer and an employee, a speechmaker, a politician—will find the proper methods of teaching applicable. This book is partly theory, but largely practical tips and advice on communication and teaching. From that point of view, anyone other than a hermit could benefit.

Finally, I think you can benefit even if you are not in any of these categories. This information can provide you with a standard of self-evaluation. If you know a proper philosophy of education, you can look at yourself and say, "How was I educated? Did my parents and teachers give me what I needed for mature life? If not, can I supply the lack, myself, now?" If you know the standard that man requires by his nature, you can begin to judge your own case and remedy any deficiency you might observe. In that sense, a philosophy of education is like a checklist for your own readiness to face the tasks of life.

The pure philosophy—metaphysics, epistemology, ethics, politics— is standard Objectivism but the application to education is my own. (I had very little discussion through the years with Ayn Rand on this particular subject. Clearly, I do not believe I have made any false applications, but I do not want Miss Rand saddled with the responsibility.) If education is instruction in the powers necessary for life, what are those powers and for what kind of life? I have to give specific Objectivist content; otherwise, the topic is simply too broad to guide us in any meaningful direction.

A proper theory of education, like a proper theory of ethics, must tell you specifically how to function on earth. It cannot be just ambiguous, floating abstractions. At the very least, it has to tell you two things: how to instruct (method) and what to instruct (content). If a theory doesn't tell you that much, it is just worthless verbiage.

Five Theories of Education

Throughout the centuries, five theories of education have been most popularly accepted by philosophers and schools. Each prescribes different answers to the questions of Purpose, Content, and Method. To formulate a proper philosophy of education, an evaluation of these approaches is both instructive and necessary. Decide which ones you agree and disagree with.

Classical Theory

Education is essentially the communication of factual knowledge. Man has accumulated vast amounts of information about reality. This information is organized systematically and transmitted during the educational process. Basically, this theory sees education as the process of giving youngsters vast amounts of information, the more the better. Cognition is necessary for mature life, and this is the power to be developed. The essential of mature life, this theory states, is knowledge of reality. Knowledge of reality is clearly a precondition of successful action.

Notice that factual information does not necessarily mean concretes only, just making the student memorize names and dates. It can also include principles of science or history. The point is to fill the students with information. It can be organized, it can be logical, it can be principled, but give him as much as you can. There is an obvious plausibility to this theory. If you don't communicate knowledge it is hard to imagine what else you could do. This is the traditional approach to education.

The test of success: How much has he learned?

Socialization Theory

Education is essentially a means of socializing the child. According to this theory the purpose of education is to train children in social adjustment, enabling them to become useful members of the group, the community, and society. The idea behind this theory is that the essence of life is one's relationship to other men. We don't live on a desert island. Every value you want to achieve involves dealing with others. Every source of human happiness or fulfillment, whether it is work or love or anything else, involves relating to others. This is what the child must learn if he is to function successfully when he grows up. And this, therefore, is the task of education. John Dewey is most prominently associated with this view.

The test of success: How well does he relate to others?

Child-Centered Theory

Education is a means of individuating the child. The purpose of education is to enable the child to discover, realize, and fulfill his own self. Behind this is the theory that every child is potentially unique and education should concentrate on bringing out this aspect, of fostering his individuality. The most crucial trait to bring out educationally is independence: train the child to stand on his own and not rely on others. The advocates of this theory (the Individuality Theory) are very opposed to the factual knowledge (Classical) theory because they claim it makes the child passive. He should be active and creative. He should do things as a unique entity, not just sit there and absorb data. Their idea is that if you focus on developing the uniqueness of the child, creativity will spontaneously well up. The philosopher, John Dewey, is a famous advocate of this particular theory.

The test of success: How independent is he?

Moral or Behavioral Theory

Education is essentially a means of developing morality in the child. Different terms may be substituted for the word *morality*: virtue, conscience, a sense of values, good character, good habits, proper pleasures, right emotions, mental health. But they all reflect an orientation to the child's psychology, emotions, and behavioral side. The advocates of this theory may differ very strongly on: "What is morality? What is a good character?" For instance, medieval religionists usually subscribed to this approach to education, as did Adolf Hitler. They had different ideas of what they wanted to turn out, but they both believed the purpose of the schools was to instill a certain kind of character in the child, and that it was not important whether he individuated himself or acquired knowledge.

The idea behind this theory is that a child is born amoral, but moral character is critical to his development, his functioning, and his happiness. He has to learn the right values and emotions. That is what will shape all of his actions and his existence. Therefore, education must focus on the development of good character. This theory of education has to be conjoined with an ethics to yield a concrete content because you have to establish what good character is. But when you combine it with an ethics, you get a very specific theory of education. In today's world, religious groups such as the Moral Majority or the Fundamentalists are most associated with this view.

The test of success: How good is his character?

Cognitive Theory

This school believes education is essentially training in methodology, specifically in the methods of thinking, of using reason, of using one's intelligence. The advocates of this view are not concerned with how much knowledge you give the child. Their focus is training the child how to use his mind and how to think critically. He can always get concrete information later, on his own.

The underlying argument is very simple. How you use your mind determines whether your knowledge does you any good or not. If you don't have the right method or you use it sporadically or haphazardly, your knowledge comes down to just so much memorized dogma, and is useless to you anyway. What counts in life is not the content that you know, but the training of your intelligence. John Dewey is the philosopher associated with this theory. This is not an unprincipled eclecticism on his part. On the contrary, it is perfectly consistent that he advocated this view and both the socialization and child-centered theories.

The test of success: How effective are his thinking skills?

Your first reaction to evaluating these five theories may be that it is ridiculous to have to choose. You want your child to know something, to get along with others, to be an individual, to be moral, and to think correctly, so why sit and agonize about which theory is the best?

The answer to this is that it may be possible to combine some of these into a principle. However, you cannot accept them all because they are the foundations of a philosophy of education, and each of these theories dictates a whole unique system of education.

We are looking for the primary, the root on which everything else is going to be built. When you are at the level of primaries, you cannot choose everything, despite the fact that some aspects may be good or desirable. There is an important analogy here to Ayn Rand's argument as to why it is a disaster to justify capitalism by saying it helps the poor, even though it does help the poor. If you make that the thrust of your argument, it implies that helping the poor is the standard of virtue. If that is so, that means you have established the altruist morality as your ruling code, and you are committed to collectivism, not capitalism. Ayn Rand's work emphasizes the crucial difference between a primary and a secondary consequence, however desirable that secondary consequence may be (such as helping the poor). That same issue applies here. Each of these theories is offered as the primary. As such, it dictates the entire approach to education, both in method and in content.

For example, everybody wants to socialize his child in the sense of teaching him to relate to and get along with others. If socialization becomes the primary, if that is the principle which is going to guide you in your educational direction, that means that relating to others is more important than training the mind or acquiring knowledge, and so forth. Under the socializing theory, the fundamental guide has to be to fit into the group. That is the fundamental and the whole educational system is planned accordingly. From this point of view, the cardinal sin is to let the child do anything alone because that inculcates bad habits in him. It weakens and minimizes the crucial power that is supposed to be developed and strengthened: namely, relating to others.

So techniques are deliberately devised to make education as social as possible. For instance, in these schools learning will occur only by group vote. The whole group votes and the child gets the idea that until the group has spoken, there is no truth. In kindergarten, when children are pre-conceptual, building blocks are too heavy for one child to lift. So a young child can't make anything by himself; he has to enlist other children in the group to build something because it is simply physically beyond his power. In grades three or four, when a biography is assigned, the data is cut up into strips and some data is given to one group and some to another. Each group must search out who has the rest of the data, and only the class as a whole can complete the biography. There are countless ways to inculcate the idea that you can do nothing by yourself. You should be able to see just some of the disastrous consequences that follow from taking a perfectly desirable, rational human trait—relating harmoniously to others—and making it a primary.

Similarly, with the individuating theory the purpose of education is to develop independence, self-fulfillment, and personal creativity. These are all positive attributes, but if you took them as the primary, what would it lead to? It leads to whim-worship, which is a desire experienced without regard to knowing or caring to discover its cause ("wishing will make it so"). Individuality precedes knowledge, cognition, thought, and reason. As a primary, it leads only to disaster. It really leads to pseudo-individualism, because once the child is not being guided by reason, he is being guided by emotion. That means he loses his actual independence, which is his own judgment and ends up accepting other people's value judgments.

What does the child-centered, individuating theory translate to in educational practice? The classroom becomes a laboratory for self-discovery.

Each student is encouraged to conceive of problems in his own way. There is no pre-set curriculum; rather, the self-motivation of the individual (his "natural quest for knowledge") directs what he wants to study. An environment is established that allows the students to pursue their "interests" through activity centers, group work, and collaborative thinking—Dewey's learning by doing. Each student draws his own conclusions through his own methods, arriving at what satisfies him at the time. Evaluation is typically reached through self-assessment or group consensus.

There are many schools that follow this particular path. It leads directly to subjectivism, the doctrine that feelings are the primary tools of cognition. It has just as disastrous consequences as the socializing theory because they are two different forms of undermining the student's mind. This is why John Dewey was comfortable with both: he could oscillate back and forth at will.

Let's consider the moral theory. Morality is not a primary; it is a derivative. Philosophically, morality is a product of metaphysics and epistemology. In each person's life and psychology, his moral character is a product of his thinking, his knowledge, and his value judgments. What would it mean to make morality a primary? Virtues are simply where you start. It means there is no validation; children just accept what they are told about good and bad. They imitate certain traits of character from others. They simply obey and do what they are told. Morality, here, is an issue of revelation and that is why this theory is so often conjoined with the religious approach. This is obviously inappropriate from the Objectivist philosophy. The essence of morality for Objectivism is thinking. That is what all the other virtues derive from, so a theory which makes good character the primary could never be accepted.

That leaves the two most plausible of these candidates as our primary: education as the communication of knowledge and education as training in the methods of thinking. Who could say that knowledge is dispensable? Man survives by his awareness of reality; that is fundamental. He survives by learning what his predecessors knew, and adding to it, so he has to learn what the context is now in order to function at all. No one can derogate the importance of the transmission of accumulated knowledge. On the other hand, the method of thinking—of using your mind—is also crucial. Reams of data are useless unless they are grasped by a thinking mind that knows how to understand, interpret, integrate, and apply—and that needs training. It is not self-evident how to think, but it is essential to life. Reason is man's means of survival and teaching the method of thought really means teaching reason.

It is impossible to choose between these two. Therefore, I happily conclude you don't have to choose because, properly understood, each of them implies and necessitates the other. These two are not like the other three theories that you can separate out as independent possibilities. It is only the proper understanding which combines these two and makes a proper educational principle. Just knowledge by itself without a child knowing the method means dogma, revelation, and blind memory—and that is not knowledge. Everybody acknowledges that much, but not everybody knows the other side: you cannot teach method by itself, either. Never, not at any point from grade zero to grade twenty-five. *Method requires knowledge.*

There is no way to teach the method of thought, except on some content. Method, as such, is empty. Thinking means thinking about something. To teach method, you have to teach subject matter, facts, information, and content—filling the student with an overabundance of the data of reality. But, just as importantly, you have to teach it by a certain means. The result is that at the same time you are giving him knowledge, you are also training him in method.

To train in method is nothing more than to present content in a certain way. It is a false alternative to distinguish between content and method, or factual information and mind training. Factual knowledge is the focus on reality. You give the child awareness of what is out there. Mind training is the intellectual process—and that is reason. So this alternative comes down to: "Should we give the child reality or should we give him reason?" That is a hopeless dichotomy. Reason is your means of knowing reality: if you divorce the two, you do not know reality and you are not reasonable.

Intrinsic, Subjective and Objective Theories of Cognition

There are two schools of philosophy, intrinsicism and subjectivism, which will make this dichotomy intelligible to you. The intrinsic theory of cognition holds that all we have to do to acquire knowledge is simply let reality act on us. It is not necessary to focus on our minds, our consciousness, our cognitive faculty, our reason—that is irrelevant. We just have to open our minds and something out there in reality will act on us and produce knowledge as we passively sit back and wait. Therefore, this school maintains that it is a waste of time to bother teaching methodology. Just pour in all the data you can and the child's mind will act like a mirror. Knowledge is simply a passive mind absorbing what reality thrusts on it. The theory of education that follows from intrinsicism concludes that all cognition is like sense perception. A child doesn't have to have any special method to see a chair: he just sits, opens his eyes and the chair acts on him. There is no need for validation or motivation. The intrinsic school holds that you sit the students in class, put the equivalent of chairs in their head, and they just absorb them.

The subjective school, on the other hand, holds that we should focus on the development of our consciousness apart from worrying about reality. What really counts is consciousness, not existence. The idea is that you can train or develop your mental processes by themselves, apart from reference to the data of reality. Consciousness doesn't need existence: it is a self-contained world we can develop. Subjectivists give two different answers when asked what should govern and determine how minds operate if it is not the data of reality. Those who answer "society" are advocates of the socialization theory of education. Those who answer "personal feelings" are proponents of the individuating or child-centered theory. That is why John Dewey had no trouble combining all three of those theories. Having dispensed with reality, he realized that they are all variants of the same thing.

If you are not being guided by reality in training the mind, then you are guided by your feelings or somebody else's feelings. This dichotomy, the intrinsic versus the subjective, permeates our whole culture. And it pervades and corrupts the entire field of education and the philosophy of education.

Neither the intrinsic nor the subjective approach results in a proper theory of education. For each of the following topics, I will demonstrate what the intrinsicist view would be, what the subjectivist view would be, and contrast those with the objectivist view. You will see how each approach affects the method of teaching and the nature of the curriculum. I use the term "objective" to stand for the approach to cognition that is neither intrinsic nor subjective. Objectivity means grasping reality by some specific human method. It means using your consciousness in certain steps, according to certain rules, in order to discover the facts of reality. And that is the essence of a proper theory of education.

So, from the objective point of view, should we teach facts? Should we give factual knowledge to our students? Should we inundate them with data from reality? My answer is, absolutely, unqualifiedly yes—a wealth of factual information. Should we wait for later? Absolutely not; now is the time. It is absurd to wait until a student has acquired a good character before he studies reality. Should we just train him in the method and let him figure out the facts himself? That is equally absurd. The essence of education is the accumulation of information about reality. There is nothing else to do or to know. And therefore, the more knowledge you teach (other things being equal), the better. That does not mean blind memory because you have to learn by a specific method and in the act of teaching you are training that method. You are training young minds to use that method. If you do it properly, you set up a virtuous circle. Every new piece of information improves the child's proficiency in the method of thinking. And every such improvement enables him to grasp new data more efficiently.

The intrinsic approach is basically the old-fashioned religionist approach. Very often, they gave good data but they never trained minds. The extreme example of that in continental Europe is the Prussian approach to education. You just pound it in; the students memorize and spew it back. The modern alternative to that in America is Progressive education which is simply the subjectivist side of the coin; namely, that reality is irrelevant. The Dewey advocates assert that each individual will develop on his own automatically if you just let him alone. He is like a coiled spring. All that is needed is to remove the restraints, prohibitions, and interference of reality and he will unwind into creativity.

That is simply nonsense. Education is needed precisely because children do *not* automatically develop. They need a system to develop their powers. It is not true that the best thing to do is just leave them alone and let them do their own thing. The deepest philosophic reason why this approach is wrong is because they have free will. A mind that has free will must be trained in correspondence to reality. It has to be educated, molded, taught, shaped, not just left alone to do its own thing. The goal of education is not freedom, certainly not freedom from reality. The goal is knowledge acquired by a thinking mind.

I am a strong advocate of a highly directive style of education. You, as teachers and parents, have the responsibility of imposing your views on every subject just as you impose that $2 + 2 = 4$. You cannot just let him "be himself."

Taught by the right method, the child will simultaneously develop morally. According to the Objectivist theory of ethics, the essence of virtue is thinking. Since you make that such a focus, his character will develop accordingly. In the act of teaching the right method and the right content, you are inherently teaching the right morality. In many concrete and indirect ways, you give the child the message of the value of integrity, honesty, productiveness, justice, independence, and pride by the way you teach the essential content. He will be independent because the essence of individuality is reliance on your own mind. The proper thinking methods will give him that confidence. He will even have the main prerequisite for being a sociable individual, which is self-esteem, and that requires reliance on his own reason.

On this basis, our definition of education is refined and complete: *Education is the systematic process of training the minds of the young, both in the essential content and the proper method.*

This formulation leads us to two questions:

- What is the proper method of human cognition?

- What is the essential content?

One word in Objectivist philosophy indicates the answer to both these questions and is the key to the entire Objectivist approach to education: *concepts*. Man gains knowledge (once we pass the perceptual level) by the use of concepts. The proper use of concepts is not obvious but that is what, above all, must be learned. Concept formation is the human method of cognition. It is a way of organizing content. In the very word "concept," you see the false dichotomy between facts and method. Concepts are organizations of data. They are ways of storing or integrating factual data. Take the word "table," which is a concept. It is a mental symbol that enables you to hold in one mental frame all the tables around the world. There are no concepts without data and no thinking without an abundance of material content.

What, then, would be the data that you want to give a child? For obvious reasons you can't teach everything so the content must be delimited to essential content. You have to be selective about what mankind knows; otherwise, you could run the entire school from kindergarten to university on what is known about worms.

A curriculum must include whatever data is necessary for the conceptual faculty to develop. Some knowledge is peripheral, such as how to drive a car. Your conceptual faculty is not impaired if you don't know how to drive. However, some data is so essential to the conceptual faculty that without it, it cannot develop. That is what the school should communicate in content. And, of course, it should communicate the method at the same time.

I think we can agree with our final definition: Education is the systematic training of the conceptual faculty of the young, by means of supplying, in essentials, both its content and method. The purpose of education is to take a perceptual-level creature, and train him across many years, so that he emerges a mature, cognitively self-sufficient, informed being. And that is the principle that dictates both the curriculum and the instructional method.

CHAPTER TWO

The Teaching of Thinking Methods

The purpose of education is to train the conceptual faculty by teaching proper thinking methods and supplying essential factual content. This chapter is devoted to how to teach thinking methods: how to teach the student the proper use of his mind. The focus is almost entirely on what to do in the primary and secondary grades. By the time you reach college your thinking methods are fairly well determined, and it is a tremendous struggle to improve or alter them. Here, we are concerned with what to do with a young child to enable him to reach the proper stage by the time he enters college.

You do not teach thinking methods by giving a course on the proper method of thought, however simplified and however well presented. You cannot sit down with youngsters and tell them the rules of deduction, the key fallacies to avoid, how to make inductions, or how to formulate definitions. That is much too abstract for their intellectual level. They simply do not have enough knowledge of the subject matter. And therefore, however well you present the rules, they will necessarily be theoretical, floating abstractions (concepts detached from reality that a student accepts from the teacher), essentially unreal to them at this age.

Extrospection must precede introspection, whether in an individual or in the whole history of the human race. First, you have to gather information. Then, at a certain level of sophisticated development, you can analyze what your consciousness is doing with this content. You can abstract the method you are using and, if necessary, improve it.

The earliest stage to give a formal course in method is the late high school years. At that point, it would merge into a course on epistemology. I do not rule out giving some tips, some logical fallacies to watch for, and so on in the earlier years, but lecturing on thinking skills should never be the primary method.

The modern Progressive alternative to the rationalist idea that you sit down and lecture on methodology is to just turn the child loose and let him explore or experiment on his own to find out what "works" in solving his problems. That is a complete abdication, because you are expecting the child to discover, on his own, the methodological discoveries of the whole human race to date. Education must be directive; you cannot just sit back and wait for nature or the child to do something.

But what is the right method of teaching thinking? It must be directive, but not by means of floating abstractions. It must be by a procession of specifically chosen concretes. The child must be taught method with concrete subject matter. You have to address specific subject matter rationally, time after time. And I mean here, literally hundreds of times across many years, instance after instance of what rational thinking consists of, so that the student is steeped in the proper thinking methods in actual daily examples.

With each new point or each new subject, the child must be getting another example of: "This is how to think. This is what is involved. This is what the mind should be doing." The teacher's role is to model proper thinking methods on a variety of subject matter over and over. If this is correctly done, the child, when he is older, will be ripe to simply abstract what the common denominators are. Teaching is a form of communicating thinking. After countless examples of good communication of thinking, it becomes very easy to abstract the common denominators, at which point the student can become an independent thinker.

I do not believe a child can become an independent thinker earlier. In a sense when he is between six and twelve, he can think on his own in a receptive sense. He can judge whether somebody's presentation or statement makes sense or not, but he cannot delve into new material and direct his mental processes to discover the new in a rational, self-sufficient way. He cannot be creatively in control until he reaches beyond this stage.

To summarize this point: to teach well is to teach according to certain conceptual principles. This very act teaches the information about method that will later be abstracted into formal thinking methods.

Principles of Good Teaching

There are three broad principles of good teaching:

- Motivation
- Cognitive Integration
- Sequence and Structure

Motivation

Man has free will. He has a volitional consciousness which begins on the conceptual level. Conceptualizing is a voluntary activity. It requires a commitment of effort, time, work, focus, and sweat—mental sweat. It can be difficult, and you must have a reason to do it: a purpose, a reward, a result that you want to achieve. There are countless possibilities of how the student can employ his mental time. Out of all those possibilities, he has to know: Why this one? What for? Those questions must be answered convincingly, or everything else is a waste of time. There is no use giving the most wonderful presentation without motivation because it simply does not take.

Motivation is a presupposition of a student having an active mind. He will have an eager interest in the subject and a desire to know, but only if he sees a value in doing so. He may stay with a subject for a few minutes, on the grounds of generalized goodwill toward cognition, but he will not persist without motivation. Every subject, however well presented has dry stretches, complicated parts, and difficulties. Counter to the Progressive propaganda, not all learning is orgasmic. Sometimes you do have that phenomenon and it is a wonderful reward, but there is a lot of buildup and foreplay. If you just shove the material at the student as a duty and say "learn this," without convincing him as to why, his mind will just wander off at the first obscurity or dry spot. An active mind has to be a motivated mind.

Motivation is also a precondition of a reality-oriented approach to any subject. You cannot be reality-oriented if you are not motivated. Knowledge is not an end in itself. It is the student's means of dealing with reality; in other words, with the actual concretes in his life. In essence, motivation consists of pointing to the concretes in reality that the child will be dealing with and showing him how he can deal with them better if he learns what you are teaching. That is the only way you can anchor a whole subject from the outset. You make every subject part of the skill of dealing with reality, as against "I just learned this stuff because somebody told me to." Learning the latter way is a guarantee of having the subject float in the child's mind, however well it is taught, and however many eloquent examples the teacher gives, because the whole subject, if unmotivated, is disconnected from his life in reality.

For example, the typical way to begin teaching the philosophy of education is to say, "Our subject is the philosophy of education. Here is the definition." Questions would arise in your mind such as, "What does this have to do with anything? Why do I have to know what it is? What would I do with it?" The result is that the subject is floating, not connected to any concretes in your life, and ultimately, you simply would not retain it.

When I provided a very brief motivation for you in the previous chapter, I tried to indicate an area of actual concretes in your lives about the decisions you must make if you deal with children. That directed you at once to the realm of life and reality.

Another thing motivation accomplishes is that it is the first step in teaching proper values. (We will see later that just as with method, so with values.) You do not teach values by abstract lecturing, but by proper concretes. And the first step in teaching the proper values is by the kinds of motivation you endorse and rely on. To motivate a class is to specify values that you are going to achieve. You actually encourage certain values in students by the kinds of motivation you offer.

For example, in the motivation that I gave you for reading this book, I was relying on the fact and trying to instill the idea that you should be responsible as parents, and that you should act independently rather than just leaving education to the school. Those were the kinds of values I was appealing to in stressing why you should know this material. A proper motivation teaches rational values. It communicates to the child: you are going to develop your abilities and your capacity to stand on your own and to judge independently, in contrast to "Learn this because society demands it," or "because you will fit in better with the group," or "because everybody's doing it," or "because I say so."

It is, of course, important that you appeal to a child's actual values, and not simply rational values that he doesn't care about. He will not react to a motivation that doesn't address values that he actually cares about. The point is you have to select out of whatever mixture he brings you, those values which are rational. You do not pander to mistaken or negative values. If he happens to have a craving for neurotic popularity, do not tell him, "Learn this arithmetic lesson because everyone will love you." That is an undesirable motivation if it is his primary one. You select what you know you can count on in him, however fragmentary, and try to appeal to that. Motivation is urgent; it is the precondition of an active mind. It is the first step in tying the child's conceptual faculty to reality, and in helping provide him with rational values.

Contrast, on this one point, the two other schools of education, the intrinsic and the subjective. An intrinsicist's attitude toward motivation is that you do not need it. Motivation is a process of getting consciousness ready to learn, preparing the inner conditions. For an intrinsicist, consciousness is completely passive; it doesn't do anything. It just sits there while reality writes on it, so it is completely unnecessary to do anything to get the consciousness ready. The teacher simply comes in and starts to dictate, and the students just swallow it.

The subjectivist side enthusiastically advocates motivation. However, their idea is to find something that the student's emotions respond to and then connect the lesson to that. That perverts the whole purpose of motivation. It makes motivation a means to whim-worship (omniscience based on emotions), instead of a means to developing rationality and a connection to reality. It is true that a child starting to use his faculties gets a definite satisfaction out of using them and, if guided in the correct mode, will continue to enjoy doing so. But it does not mean that it will be automatic, particularly when he has to learn things that he is not interested in at some stage. This is often the situation when the requirements of the content are at variance with the child's interest. It may be inappropriate to present what he is interested in because he does not yet have the background to grasp it. In such a case, you have to specifically provide the kind of motivation that will carry him through this stage until his interest naturally flows in the same direction as the logic of the subject demands.

Motivation should not be an appeal to any arbitrary value, not even if it would work temporarily in really motivating a child. Motivation is part of long-range conditioning. There are many different ways to motivate, depending on the subject and the audience. Some things to some audiences are obviously important, so only a very brief motivation is required. In other instances, students with no background, no proper training in thinking methods or a contempt for anything school-related will need significant motivation before you even think of addressing the subject matter.

You have to define your audience carefully. You must determine whether it has an established knowledge and interest in an area or not. Every subject has its own distinctive handle but it is somewhat easier to motivate the young than adults. Children are still open and intellectually flexible. Let me give you an example. Suppose someone tried to motivate me to devote the time and effort to learn economics. It would be impossible because I am so specialized in my interests. I am so integrated around one area that it would simply be impossible to blast me into the effort necessary, however eloquent the case was made. But, as a college student, I was more open to economics and wanted to know something about production and trade. I was not yet so one-track-oriented. Children illustrate the same willingness. They are not so developed in one area and are generally open to new knowledge. One real advantage you will have in motivating children is that they are aware that they do not know much of what there is to know. They are eager to emulate adults. They know they have oceans to learn, so they are relatively easier to motivate, and ripe to teach, if only you present the value of the subject to them in terms they can grasp.

The principle of motivation is this: show them that the skills they themselves want to have or might want to have depend on mastering this subject. The "might want" is critical. There are many things they do not necessarily want now but they might want some day.

As an example, suppose I am teaching literature. A natural way to motivate eight- or ten-year-olds would be through characterization. I would slow down the presentation and tell the class in appropriately simple language, "You deal with people all the time. Sometimes they disappoint you. You have to learn to figure them out, to judge which ones are good and which are bad. Can you get any clues from some traits that will help you predict others?" Or I would say, "You are growing up and deciding what kind of person you are going to be. Wouldn't it be useful to have an indication of all the different types of human beings, like a menu at a restaurant? That is really what literature is. It is like a menu of the kinds of human beings, what to expect from them and an exercise in seeing if one trait leads to another." If you work all that out beforehand, if you do not pour it on too fast, the student starts to read right away with a kind of interest in the idea that this will help him judge people, understand his playmates and decide what he wants to be. This motivation makes the act of reading more immediately purposeful than if he just reads because you told him to read.

I want to stress that motivation is not simply something you provide at the first class or the opening discussion. It must be continuous. You have to persistently refer back to your motivation throughout the entire subject matter. You have to show that you are actually delivering on your promise and achieving the value in question. If you are teaching literature, you have to repeatedly ask, "Do you want to be like this character? Why or why not? Who does this character remind you of? What did you learn about people that you didn't know before?" Motivation is a continuing responsibility that you can never abandon.

The primary factor in motivation is to effectively communicate how the developing mind will be helped in knowing this material. However,

there are some secondary factors that contribute to motivation. The enthusiasm of the teacher and his commitment to the subject is vital. This
has often been noted in manuals on teaching, and it is necessary if the
class is to get a consistent context. If the teacher eloquently explains how
important the subject is but he drones on as though it bores him out of his
mind, he has presented a naked contradiction to the young child, in terms
of both motivation and values. It makes a tremendous difference from
kindergarten right through graduate school if the teacher communicates,
"This is urgent. This is crucial. I love it; it is really exciting." If you do not
like a subject, either do not teach it or cover it up. Regard your teaching
as acting and whip up a storm of excitement. It is possible to be infectious
while inwardly thinking, "Well, it is two o'clock; I only have 57 minutes
left." All professional teachers must do this to some extent. However
much you love your subject, when you deliver a concept for the 998th
time, it is not quite as thrilling. You simply have to learn the technique
of acting as though you are delivering the material for the first time and
are relishing it. It is important to remember that this is just a secondary
factor. If you present something in the most excited manner, but the class
has no idea why, they will be baffled. In every case, you must first lay
down the actual reasons for the subject.

Another secondary factor, which I heartily endorse, is anything
reasonable that will make learning a pleasurable experience. Of course
in a general long-term way, enjoyment does accompany the gaining
of valuable information, but the problem is that the pleasure is often
delayed or interrupted by necessary and unavoidable arid stretches in
the subject. My view is that anything that will get you through those
drier stretches is perfectly sound, so long as you do not subvert the
essential presentation. That is why I am a strong advocate of humor
as part of any presentation. (I do not mean interjecting with the tired
"This reminds me of a story," as the class sits back and sighs.) If you
can make them laugh, it helps give them the idea that this process is
not quite so tedious. It also helps to keep them awake. You should not
be a perpetual comedian but as an adjunct, it is very valuable.

As part of this promotion of pleasure, I also advocate making
games out of learning as much as you can (again, without subverting
the purpose). I bless the man who taught Latin at my grade school because we learned it like a baseball game. Knowing all four parts of the
verb was a home run. It was exciting to help your team win. Games
should not be used as primary sources of motivation but within the
context of the proper motivation and presentation, I think they are

useful complements.

A child wants to exercise his powers and get an immediate reward, not just wait for the day when he will be smarter and able to function fully. So I am an advocate of competition, contests, and prizes in school. There are those who think that this is vulgar and depraved; that a child should be motivated only by the desire to know reality; that it introduces psychological corruption if he competes with others or is given a prize for his success. I do not accept that theory. Of course, I do not think awards should be primaries. The basic motive that you instill in a student should not be to beat others or win accolades, but within the proper framework, as a secondary theme, I do not think competition is harmful, and it adds a definite element of motivation and pleasure. It contributes to making school fun and allows students to show off in a perfectly good sense. It is the same desire as wanting to win a sports game. That does not make you psychologically aberrant; it is just much more fun that way.

You could even make the point that competition is an important aspect of capitalism and a form of self-assertiveness. Competition is not a dirty word. Those who support the elimination of competition fear that there is a psychological danger for the child who does not distinguish between his lack of ability to "win" and his failure as a person. That danger would exist even if there was no competition. If he gets his lessons wrong all the time, he can equally draw the conclusion that he is inefficacious, inadequate, and a failure as a person. It is exceedingly important how this is handled. Competition is only an adjunct, with the understanding that this little contest is just to help get over the rougher spots. It is not the essential way of motivating the child. A word of caution: competition can be overdone. There is a story about the Frenchman who came to an English college and asked in a perfectly casual way, "How many students committed suicide after the exams?" He was amazed to find that they did not regularly commit suicide because in France it was taken for granted that there would be droves of them.

In addition, a teacher must frustrate the student in certain circumstances. By "frustrate" I mean withhold praise or approval because he has not learned something or he has made a mistake. You cannot take the attitude that in order to encourage self-esteem (which is desirable) you tell the child, "Terrific, wonderful. Whatever you do, that is fabulous," because sometimes he does get it wrong and he has to find that out, both to learn the material and as preparation for life. You can't do that by never putting him to a test, whether competitive or otherwise. You point out his flaws in a way that includes recognition of his skills. What part did he get right? What lesson did he do well? What aspect did he grasp? He sees the material that he needs to learn and realizes that he has learned many things correctly. When you first start to teach, you are very eager to correct the student completely and when he hands in a paper, you rip it to shreds. You overemphasize because you want the lesson to stick. To avoid shattering students, always prepare the ground for criticism by reminding them of something positive.

Cognitive Integration

In general, integration is the process of connecting or relating data. It means presenting information to the child, not as discrete separate items, but as parts of a whole. The technical definition of "integration" is making a single whole out of a number of parts. Integration is the central process of human cognition. It is even a preconceptual process. We start with disintegrated sensations which are united into the awareness of entities. This is done automatically by the brain so it is not the concern of education. For educational purposes, we are talking about the integration from percepts to concepts. (For a detailed explanation, see *Introduction to Objectivist Epistemology* by Ayn Rand.)

A concept is an integration of concretes into a single new mental unit. For example, the concept "man" subsumes and integrates into one mental unit all the individual men there are, present, past, and future. We observe men and see that they are similar in certain ways as contrasted with dogs and cats. We segregate them out mentally. We omit the measurements that distinguish one man from another and unite them by one symbol. The result is we have a mental unit standing in our minds for all men. Thereafter, we can think of all men in that one unit. That is what enables us to induce. We observe some trait about a few men; we can say this is true of all men.

Concepts are mental space-savers. Because consciousness is finite, your mind can hold only so much at any given time. This phenomenon is often referred to as the "crow epistemology," that is, if you are given too many units at one time, you simply will be unable to process them and your mind, in essence, becomes temporarily paralyzed. So the human method of knowing the whole universe—the conceptual method—is to reduce the number of units, thus enabling us to hold a vast amount of information in just a few mental symbols. That is what conceptualization is.

A visual example will clarify this process:

If you see 111111111111, you just tune out and cannot retain it.
But if you see 12, you can retain it easily.
111111111111 or 12

That is integration: putting units together into a super unit. And that is the essence of human cognition.

The Greeks' phrase for integration was "the one in the many." Thales said, "All things are water." He was applying to metaphysics (matter) which should be applied to epistemology. He was not right that everything in the universe is made of one substance, but his was the correct approach and why he is called the Father of Science and Philosophy. He looked at the tremendous array of everything and said, "What is in common? What is the one element uniting all the many instances that we observe?"

Socrates was the first to actually transpose this "one and the many" quest from metaphysics to epistemology, and therefore he is the father of proper thinking. He is the one who first grasped that the essence of thought is integration, "the one in the many." He did it by trying to form definitions. He would give ten examples of justice and ask, "What is it that they all have in common?" That was an attempt at integration, putting all those instances into one definition. And that process has continued from Thales to Socrates to Einstein. Einstein was trying to find laws so universal that everything in the physical world could be subsumed under them. That investigation continues today.

What does the role of integration in cognition mean as far as education is concerned? The number one thing in your mind, once you have motivated your students, is to constantly point out and stress common denominators. Through constantly making connections, unifying abstractions, and applying general principles, you develop different ways of saying the same main point. Do not let your material sprawl into dissociated facts. Keep tying it together. Keep taking an overview. Keep pointing out: this is what binds it together. This is the one; forget the many, for now. This is the one that ties the many together. In other words, keep reducing the units. This is the essence of the conceptual method that the child needs to learn.

You have to gradually, by example, bring him to the point where he is mentally uncomfortable with a mass of unrelated data, where he has automatized the need to unify whatever he deals with mentally. It takes years to achieve that state. This is not as obvious as you might think; it is actually radical advice and the exact opposite of the intellectual fashion today. Today's anti-conceptualization precisely repudiates the "one" and insists on the "many." To give you an obvious political example, take the terrorist threats. The standard view today (whether the *New York Times* or otherwise) is: "There are so many different kinds of terrorists. It is a complicated world. There are no easy answers. We have to deal with each incident independently. There are the IRA and the Shiites and the PLO and the Muslim fundamentalists. There are so many different causes: poverty, religious fanaticism, nationalism, the impersonality of our big universities. Therefore, what can we do?"

What happens is that each concrete is dealt with according to the pragmatic decision of the moment. The proper approach would be to discover whether there is a connection among some of these events. Is there some explanation for the wave of terrorist eruptions at home and abroad? Is there some relationship among these groups? Is it an accident that they are all violently anticapitalism? Is it an accident that they erupted on a world scale, only after decades of the repeatedly demonstrating that it was a paper tiger that would try to appease everyone? Would these eruptions be possible in a different world, where individualism flourished and the United States asserted itself?

If you ask these questions, you will be very quickly led to a single unifying explanation—the one in the many. But of course, this will be denounced today by journalists as oversimplification. That is why you must try to find the common denominators in everything with your students on whatever level. I stress *whatever level*; it does not have to be a profound philosophic principle which they are unlikely even to understand. For instance, if you are teaching reading and you come across the words "comb" and "tomb," I would consider it poor teaching if you did not point out the common denominator—a silent *b*. That of course doesn't seem like a very big thing to you, but it is a major connection in the child's mind. Then, when you get to the word "knowledge," and point out the silent *k* which is just like the silent *b*, only a different letter, he is one level of abstraction up. He is making an even broader integration. You could go into a short explanation of how words were formed and why some letters are silent and why some are not. The student gets something out of this. He has noted a small feature of language and he has the beginnings of understanding how our language works.

This has to be the method and principle wherever and whatever you deal with. That is really all that thinking consists of. If one of his friends or some figure from history does something he admires or doesn't like, instead of first asking him why he admires or doesn't like the action, the first question should be: What else is it like? Is it like something else he has seen, or something else he has read? He should always be on the quest to make connections. You have to prod the student into eliciting common denominators where he would never think of doing it.

For instance, suppose you were teaching a teenager *Othello* and he had also read *The Fountainhead*. One is a Renaissance work and one is modern. One is a play and one is a novel. There are tremendous differences in philosophy and in style. But I would never point out all the differences without saying, "Do you see any two characters, one in each, that have the same basic psychology?" If you wasted that opportunity, it would be a pedagogical crime because juicy issues of integration should never be passed up. Iago and Toohey would be perfect examples to connect. Both Iago in Shakespeare's *Othello* and Toohey in Ayn Rand's *The Fountainhead* epitomize an arch-villain's malice on a grand scale. Their essential motivation is hatred of the good for being the good, although in radically different ways. But the common denominator that connects them is their unmotivated, venal desire to destroy the efficacious. Once you explain that in a properly simplified way for a child, you can ask him to consider a few things about modern art, and he begins to see that this one idea can open up a whole cultural key. In the future he will very easily grasp what modern nihilism is. That is an example of integration.

The trouble with today's world, intellectually, is that difference is *in* and similarity is *out*. In other words, everybody stresses, "This is not the same as that. This terrorist group is not that one. Look at all the differences." Thinking, however, requires you to find *what is the same*. I do not say that you should indicate that everything is the same and there are no differences, but you must focus on similarity on every level that you can. That is critical.

The teaching of reading provides a graphic example of this point. The look-say method of teaching reading is the exact reverse of the proper method because it presents disintegrated concretes, whereas phonics is the method of teaching principles, preparing the child to read everything. Today history is taught in the same pluralist, anti-thinking way. Ten causes of the Civil War that have no relation to each other are presented rather than finding fundamental principles. (I refer you to "Why Johnny Can't

Think" for a more detailed examination.) Your goal should be that every subject be one whole. To put it another way, every subject should aspire to become, as far as possible, like geometry where you could not alter one theorem without wiping out the whole system.

That is the model to aim for, so the student sees that everything is so interconnected and interrelated, that each subject is one systematic total. History, of course, is not a series of deductive theorems like geometry but it does have an inner logic, even though men do have free will. It does follow certain laws, and all of the events are interconnected. For instance, you could not have had Weimar Germany, just as it was in all respects, with the exception that the dominant art was Man and Reason Glorified, or that it had a constitution like the United States. That would have been an impossible contradiction. If you were teaching that period in history, you would have to present it in a simplified way so the student could see how it all forms part of one era with certain basic motivating premises, which integrate all the developments.

Biographically, this is the method by which I was taught philosophy by Ayn Rand: how all of Objectivism is part of one total. That is why I feel a sense of futility when people tell me, "I agree completely with Ayn Rand, except for egoism or except for capitalism, or atheism, or whatever." That just simply wipes it all out.

Within the topic of integration, a few words need to be said about memory. Memory has a bad press in the United States. It is equated with blind retention, rote absorption, and a general failure to understand. People use the word "memory" as a pejorative, claiming that a person has memorized instead of understanding. While that is clearly unfair, there is another issue here. If you are against memory, the only way to reduce the need for memory is by integration. The more you understand principles, the less sheer memory is required, because the principle will give you the means to understand and recreate the answers, as opposed to just blindly memorizing. This is obvious, for instance, if you are driving somewhere in a car. The better your general knowledge of the geography, the less you have to memorize concrete instructions. The less you know of the terrain, the more you have to rely on concretes, that is, "Turn right when you see a red post, go past three chickens, and turn left." For the same reason, it is obvious why the look-say method of teaching reading requires perpetual memory while the method based on principles, that is, phonics, requires far less.

But memory, per se, is not unnecessary or bad or only for un-principled people. Memory is necessary in many ways in any proper education. And it does not necessarily mean blind retention. You must first get some facts before you can integrate them. There is no use advising that all that is required is to connect everything by principles. Principles connect *something* and you must have the *something*. That is why, particularly in the early years, there is a great amount of material that just must be memorized.

For instance, if you are learning a language, there is no way of learning the vocabulary by principles. There are many ways principles can help you narrow the problem. If you are learning Latin, you can recognize certain words by their similarity to English derivatives, but there is an irreducible core you simply have to memorize. The same is true for dates in history. If you know some historical principles, in many cases you can recreate the approximate dates. If you cannot remember Galileo's birthday, but you know something about history and the development of science, you know that he was not a contemporary of Aristotle or Einstein. If you are studying physics, you can explain why there are nine planets but first you have to know that there are nine planets. There is no way you can infer that.

This is the value of mnemonic devices. For instance, a mnemonic scheme we learned to remember the nine planets was "Mvem Jsun P"— Mercury, Venus, Earth, Mars, Jupiter, Saturn, Uranus, Neptune, Pluto. It took about thirty seconds. Memorization is not the onerous thing that Progressive educators insist unnecessarily saddles a child and restricts creativity. It is the only way to learn the multiplication tables and the elements in chemistry, among other things.

Memory is a capacity, a skill that needs training and development. Therefore, there is absolutely nothing wrong with special exercises in it. Once, recitation of memorized material was a standard part of the curriculum and grades were assigned for accuracy. With very few exceptions, Americans are aghast when they hear this. I regard memorization as an enjoyable and valuable exercise. There are countless ways in which a good memory is a value to you, even as a thinking adult. Remembering the arguments a book presented or the points the president made in a press conference or the things you are going to buy at a grocery store are examples of concretes that even the most principled adult may want to retain. Memory is your method of doing that. It is simply impossible and needless to figure everything out.

There is one final aspect of integration that needs to be stressed. If, while teaching, you always move from the many to the one, from concretes to abstractions, from instances to principles, you will eventually end up with only one broad abstraction. My insistence on similarity is culturally conditioned because we live in a society that stresses only differences. A current leading philosophic movement is called linguistic analysis. Analysis means breaking a whole into parts, that is, seeing the differences. The complementary process is synthesis, which is considered wicked today along with system building, so I stress its importance. There have been cultures that focused entirely on similarity and repudiated difference. That is just as disastrous. It eventually leads to a philosophy of mysticism or idealism; the idea that the universe is one ineffable totality. Then you arrive at this nonsense: I am you and you are me and we both are this watch and this watch is the First World War.

My reason for stressing similarities in a tremendously difference-oriented culture is to achieve balance. The other reason is that differences are largely given by perception. It does not take much mental effort to grasp the differences between a book and a television. It just takes corruption to deny it. You have to really work to establish similarities, especially if they are not on an immediately evident level.

With that in mind, a complementary direction must be constantly kept alive, not from concretes to abstractions, but from abstractions to concretes. In other words, you draw the abstraction; you teach the student to integrate, and then the next time you see him, you start with the abstraction and ask him to concretize. Ask him to connect the abstraction to reality. Ask him to give an example of it. You ensure that he still knows what the abstraction stands for and what it applies to. Education is a shuttle. You go from concretes to abstractions, and then turn around and come back to new concretes. You must always do the one, and then correct it with the other. As an example and a test for yourself, can you give an example of integration? Can you concretize? If not or if you can only reiterate the examples I have given that means you do not have it. You have just a word; you do not have it as an actual integration of concretes. (For you, it is a floating abstraction.) You have to bring a child to the point where he is, in a sense, always dissatisfied. In other words, whenever his mind is dealing with concretes, he feels the urge to abstract and unite it into some kind of integration or principle. Similarly, whenever he is dealing with abstract principles, he feels the urge to reduce it and apply it to concretes.

This kind of shuttling back and forth, which is unique to the objective approach to education, is dispensed with by the intrinsic and subjective schools. The intrinsic school is the rationalist, floating-abstraction school, so they are generally disdainful of examples or concretes. Conversely, the subjectivists or pragmatists are only interested in concretes. They derogate the idea of commonality and integration of these concretes. Only the objective approach enables you to unite concretes and abstractions. This is really the essence of clarity.

Most people recognize that it is desirable to be clear in presenting material. What is clarity in conceptual material? Clarity is achieved when concretes are united by a concept and a concept is seen to be a union of those concretes. The two gravest breaches of clarity are: a set of unrelated instances that causes too much pressure on consciousness and a floating abstraction untied to reality.

These are the two things that leave the mind helpless. These are what people are describing when they complain, "I don't know what he's talking about." Other things such as poor sentence structure or overly rapid delivery can also impact clarity, but within the ordinary norms of being clear these are the two crucial things to avoid.

Along with motivation and integration, a third point is required for appropriate teaching and learning to take place. After motivating a class, you need to present concretes and draw the abstractions leading to a principle, the parts to be united into a whole. Then the question of order must be addressed. Which abstraction or principle should come first, and why? Which should come next, and why? Which concepts or principles should be presented in what order? Absolutely essential to thinking is not only what you do in the content of your thinking, which is to integrate, but the order in which you do it, and that is the topic of *structure*.

To summarize the three teaching practices in one sentence: thinking consists of integrating data for a specific purpose in a specific sequence: integrating data (that is the second point, cognitive integration) for a specific purpose (that is the first point, motivation) in a specific sequence or structure—the final point to consider in teaching thinking.

Sequence and Structure

Any process of thinking or teaching has to proceed step-by-step. It should be like a good movie or novel with a beginning, a middle, and an end. It has to start with something that the students can grasp by itself, something that does not require still another explanation, something that is self-intelligible to these particular students. That is the equivalent of an axiom in cognition: it is a beginning. You have to build on this, follow it step-by-step, and culminate in a conclusion.

Many people go wrong by not grasping the role of structure. There are countless points that can be completely clear, if presented in the right sequence, with the right background and the necessary preparation. These same points become unintelligible if given out of sequence, even though you give exactly the same point with the same illustrations and the same arguments. Therefore, it is not only *what* you teach to your students, but *when*. In other words, organization is critical.

This idea is one important reason why the interest of the students is not the ruling standard in preparing material or in determining a lesson. You cannot simply poll a class, find out what their urgent, burning interest of the moment is, and motivate the class by gearing your presentation to their interests. They may be following the proper structure, but it is just as likely that they are not. They may be very interested in some question for which they are not intellectually ready. They may have overheard their parents discussing something or they may have seen something on TV but that does not give them the intellectual framework to be able to learn this particular material. This is particularly true of many current events. Students have no framework to understand or interpret the material. This is a great flaw of progressive education: the idea that all we have to do is find something that the students are excited about or something from the headlines that is "relevant," and gear the material to that. Interest does not mean readiness to learn. You do want the students to be interested, but many times you have to create the interest by a deliberate motivation.

This goes equally for the teachers' interests. They are no more the standard than the students' interests. Just because you, as a teacher or parent, are passionate about a given point, does not mean that that point should come first or that it should be the base of a whole course, or even that it should be included at all.

If interest is not the determinant of structure, what should determine, in principle, the proper structure in presenting material? This is where basic epistemology comes in. The essential determinant of structure is the hierarchical nature of the subject. To elaborate: from philosophy we learn that human knowledge varies according to its distance from the perceptual level. Knowledge starts with the directly given: what we see, hear, taste, touch, and smell. That is the self-evident, the obvious, the simple, and the unambiguous. We need no preparation for that. Once you have reached the stage that you can perceive at all, you can perceive in any order, and you get it whole from your senses. We build on this perceptual level in a very definite sequence and our knowledge gradually becomes more abstract, more complex, and more general. Each new stage rests on and is made possible by the preceding one, much like a skyscraper where each story is built on the story beneath it.

To put the point another way, knowledge is not a grab bag of unrelated items. It has a definite set of relationships from the foundations and direct perception on up to the most esoteric, complicated, and advanced theories. Proper education has to retravel that structure with the student. It has to take him up the levels from the foundation, from the directly perceptual, letting him see at each point how one level proceeds from the earlier, and then take him back to the directly given. That is the only way to tie abstract knowledge and concepts back to reality.

You do not do it directly. You cannot just introduce a complex theory and then give a few examples and think you are tying it to reality. It is "floating" until and unless it has been connected by a series of intermediate levels all the way back to the directly perceptual.

For example, if you are teaching a child a simple example of a higher-level concept such as furniture, you do not do it by saying, "Furniture is this, this, and this," because he cannot get it, even though you are pointing to instances of furniture. A higher-level concept is one that you cannot get directly from perception, but only from earlier concepts. In this case, you would have to start by teaching him "table," and "chair," and "bed," and so on. Only after he grasped that much firmly, could you say, "We are going to go to another step. We are going to go to graduate school, relatively speaking, and have one term that encompasses all these different things." He could never do it until he had first conceptualized the first level. What he would probably get, if you tried to do it directly, is a befuddled feeling that some kind of big objects are furniture, but he would not make any distinction between furniture and doors and automobiles. It would just be a stew in his mind, a floating abstraction. He might learn to ape you, but it would never be actually tied to reality, because the only way to do that is through the next step down.

The teaching of mathematics is another obvious case. Arithmetic has to precede algebra and calculus; otherwise, you simply make nonsense out of the entire subject. Modern educators do exactly that. The attempt to teach addition and subtraction (the most elementary arithmetical operations) in terms of set theory is an incredible corruption, epistemologically, because it is trying to teach the elementary by the advanced. It is trying to teach the directly obvious by means of some highly abstract theory. That makes absolute hash of the subject in the child's mind. If you want to see what is going on in mathematics, read a very interesting book by Morris Kline called *Why Johnny Can't Add*. (We all steal from the original *Why Johnny Can't Read* because it is such a great title.) It is full of material about what is happening in the teaching of mathematics today that would make your hair stand on end.

One of the major corruptions in the modern approach is to collapse the hierarchical nature, that is, to take the most abstruse and complicated as the foundation and derive the self-evident from it. You will not find a better way to explode and destroy the child's mind. For example, the moderns criticize traditional geometry for not being rigorous enough. They use unintelligible axioms to deduce the standard axioms. This is a modern axiom from geometry intended for pre-ten-year-olds:

> If the points of a line are divided into two sets, such that all the points of one set precede in the order of the points on a line all those of the second set, then there is one and only one point which separates the points of the two sets.

Try and imagine studying geometry, which you know nothing about, and the teacher says, "This is where we start."

This is the reason that students end up after one class, let alone after a year, with a math phobia. That statement, if you pore over it with an adult knowledge, is true and self-evident but it seems to me to be utterly useless. In any event, it is a crime to take a youngster innocent of geometry and begin at this point. That is a violation of the hierarchical structure of knowledge so gross that thereafter you make the child uneducable in arithmetic.

This is a distinctively modern aberration. Mathematics was not traditionally taught this way. In fact, in mathematics, the hierarchical structure is rather obvious. It is the simplest subject to sequence. Every subject, every topic, every lecture has some kind of hierarchy, some kind of inner logic that is inherent in the nature of the material, and an educator or presenter or a communicator must define and follow this structure. That is the only way to keep the student and the material anchored in reality.

Logical thinking really consists of following the hierarchical structure. It is teaching logic in practice. You do not teach logic by giving a child three or ten or forty fallacies to watch out for. Nor do you teach logic by having reams of formalized rules, whether Aristotelian or à la Bertrand Russell.

Logic, in its philosophic essence, consists of asking and answering "Why?" about any statement. "What is the reason for this?" "What proves this conclusion?" "What does it rest on?" "What precedes it in the order of cognition?" To think logically is really an issue of order: one idea or fact being the basis of the next. Think of the standard Socrates syllogism:

All men are mortal. Socrates is a man. Therefore, Socrates is mortal.

That is the arch example of logic because the premises precede and lead to the conclusion. While "Socrates is mortal. Socrates is a man. Therefore, all men are mortal" is the same three units, the order is no longer of a logical structure or hierarchy, and the consequence is, it is completely confusing and unintelligible.

If you are interested in teaching the child what logic consists of, you have to repeatedly exhibit the proper structure in the material you present him. That is the central way to give a child the grasp of logic. This is a real challenge to any teacher or presenter because the order is not always easy to determine. One reason is that if you already know a subject, it stands in your mind as a complex whole, a body of information that you have already automatized in your mind as something that you just know. This is true whether you are talking about a play, a historical era, or a philosophic system; whether you are an expert in *Cyrano de Bergerac*, Weimar Germany, or Platonism. If you have followed step two and integrated the material, it is in your mind at one time as one unified total.

It may not be immediately apparent to you where to begin when presenting material. As a teacher or speaker, you have to break the whole up into its parts. You have to figure out how to take something which is simultaneous in your mind, namely, all the elements of this whole, and make it into a sequence, one after the other, so that at the end, it will be one total in the student's mind, also.

For a definition of teaching or communicating, in general, from this one perspective, I like the following: teaching is the transfer of a cognitive whole from one mind to another, by means of transforming it for a while into a temporal succession. In your mind, the subject is a completely integrated whole. At the end, in the student's mind, if it is properly taught, it will be one integrated whole. But you can't get it directly from your mind to his except by beginning with the fundamental and building sequentially to the following points. You have to make it a succession of parts across time.

This aspect is by far the most challenging and enjoyable part of teaching or communicating. It is what made me go into teaching. From the time I was young, I was excited by the experience of having a whole and trying to break it up into parts; of figuring out where to start and where to go next and how to organize it in order to make somebody else grasp it. You learn a tremendous amount from this. You have to know a great deal about the subject to determine the proper order. You have to continually ask yourself: "What depends on what? What did I have to know before to know this point? What is its logical foundation? Is this point really a fundamental, or is it a derivative, which depends on something else?" This is why teachers so often say that the first beneficiary of teaching a subject is the teacher himself. He learns more from his presentation than any student can because he has to analyze it in a kind of detail that the students do not.

To illustrate how this would occur in practice, let me demonstrate how I determined a structure for this material. First, I listed in no particular order as many key aspects as occurred to me:

- Teaching thinking methods
- Training of teachers
- The purpose of education
- A proper curriculum

I restricted it to those four. If no material comes at all, then you presumably are not familiar enough with the subject to organize lessons on it, so you should do more preparation. If fifty topics come right away, you should also quit, because that means you do not have a purpose in mind. Ideally, you want to get between four and eight units to work with.

Next, I wanted to establish some order of dependence to structure the material. I decided to start with curriculum. I realized that was not the starting point because I had to have some reason as to why this curriculum rather than another. We have to know what the curriculum is designed for so the purpose of education has to precede the curriculum. Could I start with teacher training? The question would be teaching them what, for what reason? Again, the purpose of education was necessary before I could deal with teacher training. Logically, the purpose of education would be the place to start.

The next step was to go right to the end. The question is: Of the remaining units, is there one that presupposes all of the rest, that would have to come at the end? My goal was to reduce the number of units to work with. With a beginning and an ending, there would be only two units to deal with, a very manageable situation. Logic demands that in order to train teachers you must first know in what and how you will train them:

the methods and the material. That gives us a beginning and an end, thereby leaving thinking methods and curriculum as the middle. Often in the middle there is an option. Certain things you must start with, certain things you must end with, but you can argue that the middle can often be arranged to accommodate your audience, time, resources, and so forth.

The logical starting point does not always coincide with what your particular audience needs. For example, for my readers to understand this material on the philosophy of education, I had to assume a certain knowledge of philosophy, epistemology, concepts, and so forth. The philosophy of education is an application of epistemology to a specific field (education) and without that foundation the application will simply pass the reader by. The general point is that you start with material that is understandable on its own terms to your students. It is vital to remember that every audience comes with a context. They are neither utter ignoramuses nor are they omniscient. You have to select the starting point in your structure, not according to what you know, but according to what they do. You start with what they need, while remembering that the goal is to get them past where they are, into the new material that you have. In other words, you have to know the cognitive context of your audience: What do they come to your class with and what do they not have that they must have? What ideas are going to govern their listening to what you say and their interpretation of it? What widespread errors might confuse them or inhibit them or prevent them from grasping what you say? On the other hand, what points are so obvious that it will bore them if you focus too much time on them?

I want to give you one more example of developing a structure. "Teaching Thinking Methods" includes three principles: motivation, integration, and structure. I want to demonstrate the way in which I developed and organized this material. It should be instructive because it is typical of any process of organizing.

I began by making a list as ideas occurred to me:

—you have to motivate the class
—knowledge is conceptual so it is important to conceptualize the material and derive principles from it
—you have to be logical
—every audience has a definite context
—the hierarchical nature of knowledge
—each subject cannot be completely self-contained so broad integrations must be made between one subject matter and another

—establish certainty; you have to teach the students what they know
    and that they really know it
—(the role of competition in class)
—(the role of humor)

I knew that these last two were somehow different from all of the
others, inasmuch as they are not epistemological methods of acquiring
knowledge, but I felt they belonged, so I put them in parentheses.

Many people would say now that you have the material, the way to
present it in order is just to number it. That is not an organization or a
structure. It is a preconceptual grab bag of data. This is normally what
happens when you have a whole that has a myriad of ramifications in
your mind, and you have not yet determined the structure of it. So you
just spew out whatever comes to you: major points come with minor
points, last points come first, and you just pour it all out until you have
that feeling of mental evacuation.

The next crucial step is to reduce the number of units before you even
get to structure. If you have only four, you can start immediately to determine what should come first and what should come last, but when you
have nine, it is too much to deal with. You must consolidate. You must
determine which of these units are different aspects of the same point,
until you get down to a workable number. In other words, you yourself
have to employ step two of the three steps. You have to integrate, find
common denominators, and establish connections. In this case, I began
with motivation simply because I didn't *know* where to start.

I needed to connect something to motivation that would reduce the
number of units that I had. I recognized that competition is not really a
way of learning material; it is a way of motivating. Therefore, it is just a
concrete under motivation. I realized that humor was exactly the same
thing. I could leave them aside until I prepared motivation, when I would
bring them back as examples at the end of the unit.

I questioned what the difference was between concepts and integration. What is a concept? A concept is really an integration of perceptions.
A concept is perceptions put together into a super-unit. Integration, in this
broad sense, is just putting together even bigger units. This is the same
principle whether from percepts to concepts or from whole fields to other
fields. I decided that the common denominator is really "integration."

When I looked at the remaining topics, the one that clarified it most
for me was hierarchy. Hierarchy is an issue of what depends on what.
What comes first? What comes second? That is an issue of order. Was

there anything else here that depended on order? Logic is really an issue of order. What about context? Context is where you have to start, what you can take for granted on the part of your audience, and what the beginning is. That is an issue of order.

That left certainty. Certainty is what remains in the mind of the student, if you present material to him in the right order, because each point paves the way for the next. Therefore, I decided there was really one thing uniting *logic*, *context*, *hierarchy*, and *certainty* as far as teaching thinking methods is concerned. There was only one topic, of which they were different aspects. And that was the topic of structure.

I was able to reduce my topics from nine to three. I found it illuminating that although I knew all the nine points to start with, simply to see that there were three broad issues to tie it all together, made it already more organized in my mind. Generally speaking, there is a certain option as to how many points you should reduce to. If you have only one point, that means you have not broken down the topic. Twelve points are too many because of the crow epistemology—it is just too much for the consciousness to hold. I prefer anything from three to five. Three is just the right number for human epistemology. You can hold it and yet it has enough complexity. Go with three when you can but don't force it on the material. I have given classes where there had to be five points but beyond five, I will not go. I regard my material as defectively structured and improperly integrated if I have more than five points.

After I determined the three points, I had to decide the order. Here it was fairly straightforward. Since I was teaching thinking methods, the obvious questions were: "What is thinking? What does it consist of?" Once it was down to those three—motivation, integration, and structure—the substance of teaching thinking methods had to be integration. Motivation prepares students to think, so it has to precede the other points. Structure is the form in which you present the material. So I decided the order was: motivation, integration, structure. This is just a schematic example but, in essence, this is what a teacher or communicator has to do with his material. You have to break it down, consolidate it, and structure it. Later, your audience or class will have forgotten entirely the order in which you presented it. But if you do it properly, they will retain the total because it will have become one whole in their minds.

This method has to be applied at every level of education: within a class, across a course, across a whole subject, across the entire curriculum. The principle of structure is particularly important in determining curriculum. For instance, it prohibits class discussion of nuclear warfare in early grades. Students in the early grades have no first-hand knowledge, either of the facts, the principles, or the value judgments necessary to evaluate the appropriateness or inappropriateness of nuclear weapons. They have no knowledge of science, of politics, of man, of philosophy. They have no basis to understand these issues and, consequently, if you inject controversial current events into the curriculum, it is simply blatant adult propaganda.

You would be horrified at the brazenness of the anti-nuclear propaganda that is shamelessly offered as "educational enrichment" in the National Education Association teaching guides. It is not only that these people are zealous ideologues who want to promote their views, but educationally they are presenting something intrinsically out of sequence. It is the same as presenting calculus before arithmetic. The students are incapable of thinking about it. There is nothing that the presenter can do but simply force his views down their throats. It is not enough to have a logical structure. The students have to know what your structure is, as you are presenting it. They have to know, in some terms, what your order is, where you are at any given point and where you are going.

In writing, it is sometimes considered a good principle to disguise your transitions so the reader flows smoothly from one point to the next and is carried along on the momentum, but that is very different from speaking or teaching. In teaching, your transitions should be as blatant as possible. You need to say, "That is the end of point one. Now we are going to a different point. This point has a beginning, and I am going to introduce you to it. Now I am finished the beginning, and so on." Always give this little song and dance so the class knows when to take notes, where you are, and where you are going. Remember, a good lecture has three parts:

1. You say what you are going to say.
2. You say it.
3. You say that you said it.

As simple as this sounds, it is absolutely true.

In regard to structure, there can be options within the proper hierarchy of the material. You may decide to give a principle first, and then examples, or vice versa—in other words, an inductive versus a deductive approach. That typically depends on how much time you have, how complicated the subject is, what your audience knows, and so forth. You might decide to give a cause and then its effect or the effect and lead back to its cause. You may choose to follow chronology, an obvious thing to do if you are teaching history.

In some contexts, there is no particular order. There is no reason why you have to do one thing first rather than another. The question of optional structure only occurs when all your material is on exactly the same level and there is no development from one point to the next. For instance, assuming that a particular point is already clear and you wish to give five examples, there would be no necessary order for those examples. When you do have an option, the determinant structure should be drama. Build up to what will be the most powerful, exciting, or intriguing to your audience and what will allow you to give the most emphasis and development to what really matters to you emotionally.

The final point with regard to structure is the issue of *certainty*. This is a key aspect of teaching thinking methods. Your students have to find the conclusions convincing at each stage. If you have the right structure, everything will be tied to reality, and at each point students will experience a sense of confidence and certainty. Knowledge means certain knowledge. Even if you are teaching a theory, you are communicating certainty. The evidence that leads to that theory has to be knowledge. The status of that theory is knowledge, something you know for certain. In cognitive education it is essential to give the students the conviction at each point that what they are learning is certain. Certainty is contextual and at any stage of knowledge, if you properly delimit the context, the student can be certain of what he knows at that point. Later he will see many more ramifications and factors that contribute to his knowledge. It is not that he will be more certain later; he will be certain of more, later. Certainty is like pregnancy; it does not come in degrees as probability does. You either have certainty or you do not.

This is in complete contrast to today's climate of skepticism, agnosticism, and relativism: "The more I learn, the less I know." "Nobody can know anything." "Everything is changing." Besides being philosophically wrong, this notion is lethal to thought. Why think at all, if the more you learn, the less you know? You may as well quit while you are ahead, with blissful ignorance. There is no motivation to think, if you can't acquire knowledge by it. How can you think, if there is no method of thought? The educational establishment has turned skepticism—the view that you can't have knowledge—into a religion. They proselytize for this religion in school systematically, in a way that makes an old-fashioned religious fundamentalist seem to be fair-minded, impartial, and rational by contrast. These zealots of skepticism openly say that their purpose is to inculcate confusion and doubt. One of their chief methods is to present conceptual material out of order, so that there is no way for students to decide what the conclusions are (as in the nuclear situation). They cannot judge or know, and so they inevitably come to the conclusion that it is all a matter of opinion; nobody can know anything. If I had to name a recruiting method for skeptics, it would be teaching children by the anti-hierarchical method. The purported theory behind this practice is that when individuals are convinced of how little they know, they will be stimulated to search for knowledge.

Of course, the exact reverse is true. When you realize that after all these years, you have learned nothing or you are brainwashed into the idea that you are ignorant, you simply give up. If you want to do one service for your students, you have to take a stand and say, "For the reasons I gave you, on the basis of the facts I outlined, this is the truth."

To conclude this topic, it is instructive to contrast intrinsicism's and subjectivism's viewpoints on structure. For intrinsicists, each point is self-evident. Consciousness does not have to go through any process to learn; it simply passively receives what amounts to revelations from reality. You do not require any processing, any digesting, any understanding, or any order. The teacher, God, the textbook, or the encyclopedia said it, and that is good enough. Structure simply has no significance to an intrinsicist.

For a subjectivist, anything goes. Everything is based on feeling; no logical order is necessary; you do what you want. When you eventually lose confidence in your feelings because they have no basis, you end up looking to society's or some authority's feelings.

Both of these schools, the intrinsicist and the subjectivist, end up in authoritarianism. They do not say, "Accept this because logic and reality require it," but "Accept this because an authority (whether society or God) requires it."

This modern attitude toward the impossibility of reaching certainty permeates educational thought. Even seemingly well-meaning advice given to students undermines the need for certainty, and you get this phenomenon: "It's not always easy to tell what's true, but if you find the same information in three different places, it is safe to use it." This kind of training strands the students intellectually, making them easy victims of any authority or popular whim, including those on the Internet.

That is why, if you are interested in fostering individuality and independent judgment, you must advocate Objectivism. Only that will give the student reality as a basis for his judgment, inspire his confidence, and wean him away from conformity, authoritarianism, and skepticism.

CHAPTER THREE

A Proper Curriculum

W e now know in general the purpose of education and the methods of thinking that we want to communicate. But what is the subject matter that we want to teach? This is answered by the development of a proper curriculum.

Mankind has massive accumulated knowledge. You cannot teach everything. You can only teach a tiny fraction of the total: only a few essentials—even in ten years—that will equip your students for thought and for life. What are those essentials? *The Art of Teaching* by Gilbert Highet has an interesting passage on how children were taught in the Renaissance:

> The first point is that teaching began early. Children were sent to school almost straight from their mother's knee, and from school they went on to college four or five years earlier than we do. . . . They did learn more, earlier, and more concentratedly than we do. When the child went to school it was not given colored blocks to play with, and supervised in bodily co-ordination (*Subsection 4—Skipping the Rope*). It was given a copy of the alphabet and taught how to read and write. It began to learn foreign languages and to study the Bible soon after it could read. Shakespeare, who got an average small-town middle-class education, began Latin about the age of seven. Milton . . . was put into Latin by his father at seven and into Greek at nine. . . . The subjects were more limited in number, so that the energies of the pupils were not dissipated.

I strongly advocate the Renaissance approach—early, selective, and concentrated. Although *when* to teach is not a topic of a curriculum, I do favor early learning, the earlier the better. A child's general education should start around four years of age and be completed by the time he is fifteen.

What I am going to outline is not necessarily the proper curriculum for every conceivable student because students vary in a number of factors that will affect the curriculum. For instance, if a student's intellectual capacity, for whatever reason, is not up to par, then there is only so much you can teach him. Students also vary tremendously in the motivation they arrive with. Some are already neurotic. By the time they start school, it may be beyond the skill of any teacher to motivate them. They should have some appropriately delimited program. On the other extreme, their motivation may be so developed along one line at the very beginning, that it is simply absurd to give them a general education like everybody else. For instance, if you had a child prodigy (this usually occurs in the arts) whose interests, capacities, and abilities were already well formed, and whose whole life revolved around his particular talent, he should not spend the next ten years devoted to this curriculum. He could still benefit from some kind of education because he must be literate. Let him follow his own road but give him guidance whenever it is needed. In the early years it is hard to identify a certified genius so in the absence of overwhelming conviction, this student can begin a proper general education with no harm done.

What we are addressing is a general ability and a healthy motivation that is not yet so specialized as to dictate a different course of study. We are not concerned with vocational training or highly specialized advanced training. We want a proper curriculum for a general education for the general student. We need to know what the optimal curriculum should be to develop his conceptual faculty.

We are not concerned with college education, which should be highly elitist. College should be attended only by scholars and members of highly specialized professions, like medicine or law. I believe that a proper education in grade school would achieve much more for the general public than getting an M.A. in the best college today ever would. You do not need millions of courses across decades and decades. That is a modern absurdity. It is the result of a worthless, self-perpetuating educational bureaucracy. Even with the explosion of knowledge, you can give people a proper, thorough education by the time they are a normal high school graduate.

The main problem with defining "curriculum" is that it must be rigidly delimited. Time is finite. The child can learn only so much in the periods at his disposal, and if a subject is to be of any value, it must be explored leisurely in depth. Modern education delivers lightning-like "surveys," which are masses of disorganized data thrown at the student from dozens of fields and then forgotten. This is completely useless and harmful. It overloads the circuits. The idea from the Renaissance was much better. You take a few crucial subjects and study them in depth. Teachers really teach and students really learn to think in those areas, thereby training minds and building a foundation. Nothing else does. This, then, requires a rigorous selectivity regarding the curriculum.

There is another reason for delimiting. Every subject that you teach implicitly conveys a value message to the students. You are saying, in effect, "Given our limited time, this is important to know, as important as the other things you are studying." If you teach folk dancing as a subject on a par with mathematics, you are giving a deadly message to the student—what I call "cognitive egalitarianism." You are really treating serious subjects with implicit contempt. You are saying that every subject is no more worthwhile than folk dancing.

To illustrate, this is part of a newspaper survey of subjects taught in Dallas: Physical Education, Music Performance, Driver Education, Co-operative Education, Health Education, General Shop, Training for Marriage, Vocational Home Economics, General Plastics, General Ceramics, General Jewelry, and General Leather. There were also courses for credit in School Newspaper, Yearbook, Football, Cheerleading, Drill Team, and Creative, General, and Advanced Photography. This kind of curriculum is the death of education, the complete end of it. The moral to be drawn from this is: just because you like a subject does not qualify it for the curriculum. Just because a subject has some value, like driver education, it does not follow that it should be included. There should be a clear division between the essential work of education and the frills and extracurricular material which can be offered if there is enough time.

The Three Rs

Education is a very specific process: training the conceptual faculty. Only those subjects essential for that purpose should be included. To achieve this purpose, a proper curriculum requires only reading, writing, and arithmetic (the three Rs) and four other subjects.

This means, to put it negatively, a tremendous impoverishment of the curriculum. For our purposes each subject will be related to a conceptual education, to show its place therein. This will demonstrate why each subject was included and how, if properly taught, it relates to the definition of education that was given at the outset.

The three Rs are obvious. Reading is intimately tied to writing. The most important thing to read is your own writing so reading is a necessary adjunct to your own writing. But, beyond your own writing, reading is really the key to entering the conceptual world. It is the means of independent access to the accumulated knowledge and ideas of the whole of human history. As such, it is indispensable to every other subject and to practical life in a conceptual society. If you cannot read, you are to conceptual knowledge like a blind man is to the visual world. You can perhaps take a few halting steps under the guidance of some literate seeing-eye dog, but you are essentially helpless. The phonics method (not the look-say method) is the means to teach reading.

The second R, arithmetic, is the study of numbers and basic operations. A child learns to count as he learns to speak. Thus, arithmetic is literacy in relation to numbers. Without it, a child is deprived of an indispensable aspect of the conceptual faculty and horribly hampered in practical life as well.

The third R is writing. Writing is widely misunderstood and not appreciated by the educational community. Writing is taught in something called English classes. Generally speaking, you are regarded as a writer if you can sign your name, form sentences, and write a thank-you note to your uncle. I have in mind a much broader concept of writing: writing as a tool of life and thought that is not restricted to English classes. Writing is a skill that is essential to every subject and is a continuous part of the curriculum. This is writing in the sense of composition and every subject, even mathematics, should include massive amounts of writing.

There can be a separate English department to teach certain rudiments, such as grammar, punctuation, and spelling, but writing should not be the monopoly of any one department or subject matter. Every student should be given two grades on every paper and in every course: one on the factual content of that subject and the other on his ability to express it in writing. Every teacher should be a teacher of English.

Writing is not just for writers or professional intellectuals. It is a necessity of mind training, a necessity of learning the proper use of concepts, a necessity of learning exact, logical thought. It is impossible to organize your thoughts on any complex subject without the use of written formulations. There are too many aspects to any complex thinking process to enable you to identify them and keep them separate orally. You must get your thinking in front of you in some shape that you can hold and slowly review and study from different aspects. The reason for this is that the human consciousness cannot assimilate an unlimited amount of information at any one time (see the crow epistemology). When you say something aloud, you cannot scrutinize it from all those aspects at once and still retain it.

Practically speaking, when you want to subject your thought to analysis, you have to ask many questions of logic, context, and integration. Did I establish the context? Did I assume too much? Does my argument really hold water? Does this point follow from the preceding? Is this the best wording? What are my key points and how do they relate to one another? Can I see other connections among my points? Is my knowledge really certain or only probable? You cannot hold all this in your mind. The way to do it is to get some ideas and an organization written down. Then you query, you scrutinize, you check, you evaluate and you rewrite. The rewriting (editing) is not just for other readers; it is primarily for yourself because it is the process of making your own thoughts clearer, more logical, and more exact. You constantly say to yourself: Do I know the definition of this term? Is this claim really justified? Why did I use *this* word? What does this passage add? What is the relation between this example and that?

That is what rewriting consists of: answering those questions and revising accordingly. Essentially you are checking the quality of your thought. You cannot distinguish between perfecting your thinking and perfecting your writing. Editing or revising your writing is the process of perfecting your thinking and there is no other way to do it. Ayn Rand first thought out *Atlas Shrugged* thoroughly. She had very detailed, extensive notes and written formulations of all of her key points. She rewrote every single page five times. That was not only for style, but also for thinking. Every reformulation made it clearer to her. It included relationships she had not seen before and exhibited new aspects to her.

Editing, in that sense, is thinking. It gives you the chance for precision, clarity, and logic that is not achievable in speaking. Today, because there are arbitrary rules of writing, people think that you just blurt out something that is clear to you and then revise it. This reveals a fundamental lack of understanding of what thinking is.

I am the staunchest advocate of essay writing in every subject. I think every teacher and every parent has to be an editor, in this sense. You must check the thinking quality of the student. I am not speaking just of formal grammar; I am speaking of actually subjecting the student's thought processes to analysis.

The best way to teach is one-on-one, not in the form of presenting the material, but in going over the student's writing. That is the way I learned the most. I learned philosophy by going through that process with Ayn Rand. I would hand in drafts of articles or sections from *The*

Ominous Parallels, and she would just disintegrate them. She would say, "Why this?" and "How did you get here?" and "What about this jump?" and "What are you assuming there?" and "Do you know what this implies?" You should not subject a youngster to that kind of relentless surgical probing because you will petrify him. It has to be undertaken according to his ability and you have to feed him the appropriate praise, but there is no educational method comparable to this.

Here are two tips which will help when you teach writing in this way:

1. Do not just assign a topic. Help the child with the exploratory thinking. In other words, delimit the topic with him so that he does not take on something so huge that he flounders hopelessly. Discuss possible structure with him. Which points should come before others? What kind of interconnections could be made?

2. When the student submits a piece of writing, take it seriously. Always treat it as though it was a published work, from grade one up. Never treat it as just another school paper. Be very serious, frank, and blunt, with the understanding that you must not discourage or demoralize him. You have to treat it as a religious exercise, as something crucially important. This is the only way the student will learn the importance of intellectual rigor. The typical way of going over these papers is to put a few grammatical comments in the margin, and then write "fine," or "good self-expression," or some other meaningless comment at the end. That simply teaches contempt for the whole process.

I am often asked about the Montessori approach to education and generally I am favorable to it. The methods and curriculum used in the early years, from two through six years, wonderfully train the young mind to reach the conceptual level and acquire the life skills that are necessary. Her method is very well organized, flowing from the perceptual to the conceptual level. The single most brilliant feature is the idea of teaching writing before reading because it makes reading seem an automatic, self-evident consequence.

I am not an advocate of Montessori past a certain age. Conceptual training, with all of its requirements, should start early so I see no merit in continuing on the perceptual level after age six or seven. At that age there is limited value to what is called "materializing." It is fine to have blocks and charts early, but they are not needed after a certain age. You need concretes but that does not mean they have to be visual or tactile. Also, I do not advocate what is called "freedom in education," even freedom within structure. The more conceptual the material, the more sequence must take over. I am uneasy with the idea of children following their own direction after having learned a principle. In conceptual material, they are simply too ignorant; they do not know where to go. My understanding is that there is more latitude for the child to proceed on his own before he is ready than I would countenance. Further, I do not like the idea of a child doing his own research. He needs someone to spoon feed him. Tell him the principles and give him the framework. Research is a later phenomenon. In my view, Montessori is very good at the outset, but later a purely conceptual form of teaching is what is important.

In addition to reading, writing, and arithmetic, the four subject areas that are essential to a proper curriculum are developments of the three Rs.

Mathematics

Mathematics is often described as the language of thought. It is the science of measurement. Concepts, by their nature, involve a form of measurement so there is an essential tie between conceptualization and measurement. In both there is one essential common denominator. You are bringing the whole universe within the scale of human cognition. You are taking a vast complexity that is perceptually ungraspable and reducing it to a manageable, comprehensible sum. That is the essence of what they both have in common. An example is how we measure the distance to the sun. It is ungraspable on the perceptual level. You cannot make anything of it; it is unknowable. What we do is take the most gigantic unknowable quantities, and make them observable and graspable by reduction to the perceptual.

That is exactly what the conceptual process is. Take "man"—meaning all men, past, present, and future. That is a totality ungraspable on the perceptual level. You simply cannot take it in. But you can implicitly measure those that you can perceive, that is, compare them quantitatively on a continuum. You take a few: one is taller, one is shorter, one is fatter, one is thinner and so on. Appropriately done, you omit the measurements, and you thereby form the abstraction "man," which brings the whole totality into your knowledge. (For a detailed analysis, I refer you to Ayn Rand's book *Introduction to Objectivist Epistemology*.)

Properly taught, mathematics should be a blueprint of the use of the conceptual faculty. It should be like a stripped-down version of what all conceptualization is. If it were taught this way, there would be no question of motivating students to learn the subject. If the teacher introduces algebra to a beginning student with "Now we say X and Y instead of five and six and we have many mysterious rules and equations," he has made the study of mathematics unintelligible, unmotivated, and purposeless. But if the teacher introduces it by comparing the relation of concepts to percepts and higher concepts to lower concepts, then the student sees that algebra is related to arithmetic and to perceptual data in exactly the same way. In other words, we see this table, that table, that table, and we have the concept "table." We add the concept "chair" and then we have the higher concept, "furniture." In the same way, we have this concrete, and that one and that one. Then we abstract numbers: five, six, and seven. We go to a unit like "X," which stands for all the numbers: five, six, and seven. So an "X" is to five, six, and seven just as "furniture" is to "table" and "chair."

If it is taught that way, the students see what we are really doing is an X-ray of the nature of thought; the pure method of unit reduction, with the content abstracted away. Students will necessarily have respect for mathematics and an illumination of the whole conceptual process.

This requires teaching mathematics in relation to reality, the physical world, and real concretes, not as floating abstractions. In fact, mathematics should be taught in conjunction with real problems in science and engineering. The student should learn from mathematics how measurement actually opened up the whole physical world to us, how it laid bare and exposed laws that we otherwise could never have grasped. Mathematics should be taught as the key to understanding the universe, along with being invaluable training in conceptualization, not as a meaningless exercise breeding math anxiety.

There is one more related value to mathematics. It is the clearest example of logical rigor. Every subject is logical, but mathematics, as a purely deductive structure, is the most obvious example of it. In the whole curriculum, it is the best single example of structure, integrating teaching methods and content. It is no accident that Aristotle formulated logic on the basis of the mathematics that was known at his time. A student who grasps a proof in math gets invaluable training in rigor, precision, and logic, which he cannot get elsewhere. There are many questions about how much mathematics to teach. For the general student, at a minimum, algebra and geometry should be taught. A mathematician would have to convince me that trigonometry and calculus can be taught at a certain age, that they do not take away too much time from the curriculum, and that they add considerable value.

History

The second of the four subjects in a proper curriculum is history. History, in this context, is the study of man through his past actions. Observe that at least half of all cognition is the study of man in some aspect, that is, the humanities and the social sciences. This is necessarily so. A man has to discover who he is in order to be able to think properly. He must have some self-understanding and some grasp of the nature of man, or he will be unable to choose his actions and values or live his life. In that sense, without some knowledge of himself, his faculty of consciousness would be cut off from directing his actions, which means that he would be cut off from reality.

History is the subject that will best introduce the student to the whole realm of the humanities and social sciences, the best entry to the study of the nature of man. All the other humanities and social sciences are too abstract and theoretical for the early years. For a young child, they are necessarily floating. He has no factual basis yet to tie them to reality. For example, you could not teach political theory properly to an eight- or twelve-year-old because he has no way to judge or evaluate competing theories. There is no real content yet in his mind for such terms as "freedom" or "tyranny," or even "government." He has no idea what alternatives are possible or what the results were of those that have been tried so far.

First, he needs facts: What are governments? What kinds have been tried so far? What did they lead to? He needs an array of factual data before he can theorize and evaluate competing theories. Otherwise, political theory is simply adult propaganda beamed at helpless children. This is also true for economics and philosophy in the early years. To lecture on economics or philosophy before the midteens is much too abstract. It has no reality foundation yet in the students' minds.

Philosophy, economics, and politics are on the highest levels of the hierarchy. They are too far removed from a child's range of experience. To study philosophy, you need to know something about man. And that is what history gives you. History does not give you the theories; it tells you what has actually happened.

I was always puzzled by the fact that Ayn Rand majored in history in college. Why would she care what men had done in the past? As a moral philosopher, her concern was with what men should do with right and wrong. She said, "How am I supposed to know what men should do, apart from the facts of human nature? For that I have to study actual men, what they did and what the results were."

I rejoined, "Why not just study the men around you today? Who cares what happened centuries ago?"

She finally made this point clear to me. She said, "How will I know what facts represent man by his nature, and which are mere historical moods or fashions? If I look around today there is tremendous evidence for the desire for conformity. I know it is not true because I know there were the Renaissance and the Enlightenment. I know what man was like in a different era, and therefore I am able to abstract what is the essential that runs through all eras and conditions, and what is just a local variation. I can see what endures. I can discover which causes lead to which effects regardless of current fashions. I know what represents a principle, and what is just a chance variation."

She convinced me that history was a prerequisite of value judgments—and a prerequisite of all theory and evaluation in the humanities. History is, in effect, the workshop for all humanities and social sciences, including philosophy. It is the factual base; it gives us the spectrum of what has been done, what has been proved to be possible and impossible. Thereafter, you have a real basis to theorize.

History, properly taught, does not mean charts of names and dates. It does *not* mean: When did the Babylonians start and end? Where did the Egyptians come in? What are the twelve causes of the Civil War? History has to be the study of principles, and it ultimately should reveal to the student the role of basic factors in shaping human life, the role of ideas, and the effects of different ideas on different societies.

You do not start off preaching that; you reach it inductively by giving students the data. But ideally, what emerges at the end of a properly structured world history course across ten years is that there are certain fundamental ideas. They shape the political and cultural institutions of a society, and that has certain practical consequences. Some societies disappear and some prosper. History has to be taught as an issue of logical connection, not as accident. Each fundamental paves the way for the next level of practicality, as each society paves the way for the next. If you teach it that way—as an example of sequence and of structure—it will certainly be relevant to today's world. Relevance is important but it is not achieved by teaching controversial current events. It is achieved by teaching historical principles that are applicable to all eras. If students know the morals of history, you do not have to worry about their views on nuclear weapons.

If you teach history properly, you will also be teaching integration because you will be connecting the different aspects of a society. You will be teaching logical sequence and structure, and all of the material for philosophy, without ever uttering those broad abstractions. Further, you will be giving them an invaluable lesson in values, simply by showing them the results. History teaches values the same way putting your hand on a hot stove teaches values. One decent lecture on the facts of the Middle Ages versus the Renaissance will instill more values in your students than twelve lectures on "Virtues and Vices."

History has a very bad press in America. Everybody thinks it is boring and irrelevant, and of course it is taught abysmally. It is not even taught chronologically anymore which is as perverted as you can get. But in a properly taught curriculum, history is an essential subject.

Science

Mathematics teaches pure method. History gives the students the facts about man. Science gives them the facts about nature. In effect, science does for existence, what history does for consciousness. History gives students the data for what one day will be ethics and politics; science gives them the data for what eventually will be metaphysics, the nature of reality. Both these aspects are necessary for a man's intellectual development. Man acts in nature, so he not only has to know man, he has to know nature. If he does not know something about reality—what he can expect of the world, what it demands, or how to deal with it—he is necessarily helpless.

You have to bring together the humanities and the sciences. It is a disastrous dichotomy to have the two of them confronting each other with hostility and suspicion. They must be integrated. From science, man has to find out in the form of concretes that it is a lawful universe of cause and effect, that there are no miracles, that it is an intelligible world, that it is open to reason to understand.

I do not believe the purpose of teaching science is to enable the student to learn the scientific method. In other words, I do not believe that it is primarily for epistemological purposes that we learn science. All subjects equally teach epistemology if they are taught properly; one is not more logical than the others.

I do think there is value in training a child about specifically scientific methods, such as experimentation and quantification, but they should not be a major focus because you are not necessarily training future scientists. What you want to train are thinkers. The scientific method is of value only as an example of the broad methods you are teaching in every subject: precision, evidence, and structure.

Science is a crucial means of teaching the child integration. Correctly presented, you teach him connections and principles, not random facts or disconnected experiments. Only that will communicate a cause-and-effect universe and proper thinking methods at the same time. You have to teach him inductive laws and explanatory theories, not just a plethora of disconnected data. You cannot give the theories before the data, but you must give the theory. You must show him the power of the mind to condense reams of otherwise disconnected data. The whole message that he should get from science is that this vast sprawl of factual observations is brought into one comprehensible total by a few principles or by a brilliant theory. That is the one in the many. That is exactly the integration he has to learn.

The atomic theory is a tremendously valuable thing to teach because of the range of observable data that it subsumes and integrates. Copernicus is a wonderful thing to teach because of the way it simplifies a whole range of observations around one heliocentric theory. It is invaluable to teach a child, at some appropriate age, the progression from Brahe to Kepler to Galileo through certain observations; to integrate those observations by teaching certain laws of planetary motion and then integrate those into broader laws, until you finally get to Newton.

Thus, the whole subject is integrated and illuminated and the child gets the incomparable experience of actually bringing order out of chaos, principle out of concretes—and the one out of the many. Scientific history is an important way to teach science because it is not accidental. It is determined by the hierarchy of knowledge. It is the most rational field there is because you build knowledge on knowledge. You do not throw out the old knowledge; you incorporate it with the new. As an integrating device, the history of science is uniquely valuable; much more so than the history of any other field. Compare this approach with how Newton is currently taught (if he is taught at all) without any historical background: "Newton discovered that there were three laws of motion. Please write these down . . . ." It is utter disaster to teach science in this way. A student should emerge from a science program, not with the idea of how complicated reality is, but of how simple it is. Science should not be a survey of chaos, but an introduction to principles.

Which particular natural science best achieves this introduction? The curriculum should be essentially organized around physics. The rest of the natural sciences are in various ways dependent on physics or highly specialized and do not, therefore, lend themselves to exactly what you want from science teaching. For instance, astronomy is really just observed data. I do not think astronomy should be stricken from the curriculum. After all a child lives in this solar system, so he should know something about it. He is a living being so he should certainly know something about biology and evolution. He lives on earth so he has to know something about geology and chemistry. Whichever science you choose, it should always be related back to basic scientific principles and theories, within the limits of the child's ability to grasp, and that means taking them all back, ultimately, to physics.

Literature

The last of the four subjects is literature, by which I mean the sum total of world literary fiction: epics, novels, plays, and poems. This is distinguished from the formal teaching of English language, which properly is part of "writing." The selections should not be dominantly contemporary. A child should get to know, across his education, the great works from representative eras and cultures, from Greece to the present. Literature has to be taught according to the ability of the child to cope with the language, and if necessary in the earlier years, through simplified excerpts with the teacher explaining the contexts. In whatever form he learns it, the child by the midteens should have familiarity with the high points from Homer to the modern era, including—but not limited to— Shakespeare, Greek plays, French Romantics, and British poets. This kind of study of world literature is an invaluable supplement to the other subjects. A proper education is impossible without it, and it provides excellent training for the conceptual faculty.

Literature is one of the fine arts. Art is not a frill, but an essential need of a conceptual being. It is a concretization of philosophy. It is the form in which man holds philosophy in his consciousness and is influenced and guided by it. It is what keeps philosophy real. Philosophy is the theory, the abstractions; art is the model builder, the engineer. The difference is contained in the difference between an abstract lecture on rationality and independence and reading *The Fountainhead* and getting the image of Roark. It is the difference between a seminar on the Renaissance and viewing the Sistine Chapel.

What history is to ethics and politics, what science is to metaphysics, art is to philosophy. Art is the data and the concretes of philosophy in specific, easily graspable terms. If history opens up the study of man, and science opens up the study of matter, art opens up man's view of the universe as a total. It gives the student the ultimate integration—man in relation to man, within the universe. In this sense, art is the ultimate integrator of the curriculum. Philosophy is the ultimate integrator of knowledge, but in the early years, we do not deal with broad abstractions, we deal with concretes. Art gives the child concretes—the observable data that perform this broad integrating function in a form that he can grasp. Art unites history and science.

One art, therefore, is essential as part of the curriculum. One reason for choosing literature over painting or sculpture or music is that the other arts are less teachable. The major reason, however—from an educational point of view—is literature's tremendous advantage as the conceptual art. Its medium is concepts. For that reason, it is not only easier to teach but it offers the most to a potential thinker. The other arts capture a view of life too, but they do it in perceptual terms, giving you only certain broad essentials. Literature can capture subtle details, variants, and alternatives with a range and scope that is unique.

Furthermore, in the act of reading literature, a student learns directly about the use of concepts, about concepts as vehicles for the expression of thought. This is crucial whether you intend to be a professional writer or not. Thought involves competence in writing. Writing, which reflects the quality of your thinking, is significantly improved if you steep yourself in literature.

A broad exposure to the skilled, evocative use of concepts and an analysis of how literature achieves precise cognitive and emotional effects is invaluable training for your own use of concepts. Even though you may not want or need a literary style like Shakespeare or Ayn Rand, I still maintain that a study of it will improve your own writing on any theme. It will improve your precision, clarity, and proficiency at using words to express your own thoughts.

There is another important difference to studying style in literature versus any other art. You may know everything there is to know about style in painting, but since it is a perceptual thing, it will not necessarily redound to improve your conceptual use. But literature, properly taught, is actual training in the precision of your conceptual faculty, so it is an aspect of language study, that is, of concept study. Literature's union of concepts and art makes it indispensable in a proper curriculum.

Many derivative values flow from this literary foundation. Literature is a perfect introduction to philosophy. Because it is philosophy in concrete form, it gives you philosophy more directly than any other subject. It is crucial in teaching values. It is a supplement to teaching values through history because now the student is not restricted to only the historical views of concretes. He can expand his evaluation to include types of characters, situations, and possibilities that never have existed. Because of the capacity of literature to stylize and emphasize, he can now get an idea of what could exist.

Ayn Rand makes this point in "Art and Moral Treason" in *The Romantic Manifesto*:

> The major source and demonstration of moral values available to a child is Romantic art (particularly Romantic literature). What Romantic art offers him is *not* moral rules, not an explicit didactic message, but the image of a moral *person*—that is, the *concretized abstraction* of a moral ideal. It offers a concrete, directly perceivable answer to the very abstract question which a child senses, but cannot yet conceptualize: What kind of person is moral and what kind of life does he lead?
>
> It is not abstract principles that a child learns from Romantic art, but the precondition and the incentive for the later understanding of such principles: the emotional experience of admiration for man's highest potential, the experience of *looking up* to a hero—a view of life motivated and dominated by values, a life in which man's choices are practicable, effective and crucially important—that is, a *moral* sense of life.

Literature also supplements the factual knowledge of history. To gain knowledge of a period, there is nothing quite like reading its art works. And finally, properly taught, literature is an immediate pleasure which no other subject is. It is consumption in a sense no other subject can be. Its stories, adventures, plots, heroes, and villains give the message that learning can be fun. A curriculum as heavy as the one I am advocating has to be lightened in every way possible. In that sense, a little dose of melodrama is most welcome.

This, then, is my ideal minimum curriculum: *the 3Rs, mathematics, history, science,* and *literature*. It is not wrong to teach other things provided that they are hierarchically prepared, and they do not take time or focus away from the urgent subjects. Extracurricular activities which are not given the dignity, time, or emphasis of the curriculum can be present in peripheral form. Finally, remember there are countless places to learn besides school, so not everything worth learning has to be taught in a curriculum.

Art and music are ideal for learning at home. In school, they have to be taught as adjuncts to some other subject. For instance, you may study the literature of a period, and then present a quick survey of the art and music of the time, but it cannot be the focus or you will dilute the child's understanding. Art and music could be an adjunct to history as well, but they are not essentials. They are peripheral to conceptual development.

I do think there is a real value to learning one foreign language. The problem is that learning a second language and acquiring fluency in it is not accomplished in today's schools. All of the time spent on language training in the schools is simply an utter waste. If it is not possible to teach it effectively, without taking away significant time from other subjects, send the student to Berlitz or to Paris for the summer. Either way he will learn more in a month than he would learn in school in ten years.

Philosophy is much too abstract to teach at this level. If a student is not going to go to college, a brief introduction and survey in his last year of high school is enough so that he can pursue it on his own if he wishes. Similarly, all of the humanities that we learn in college—political science, economics, psychology, and so forth—should be reserved for the last year. Today there is very little to teach with regard to psychology in terms of legitimate theories. A whole science is needed before it can be given a place in the curriculum. Religion should be taught as an influential factor of history.

The whole vocational axis—shop, manual training, home economics—is a complete waste of time because it has nothing to do with conceptual training or cognition. Insofar as these skills are desirable, they should be learned on one's own or from an employer, not from a teacher in school. Physical education, the Greek ideal of a sound mind in a sound body, is a waste of time in school, time that should not be taken away from the core curriculum. If you want to break up the hours of sheer concentration required of the student, do it at recess, not as a curricular subject.

Driver training, sex education, health, citizenship education, drug abuse education, and so forth, severely overload and adulterate the curriculum. If you want your child to drive, teach him yourself or enroll him in a class. It is a complete corruption to put learning to drive and "just say no" in the same category as mathematics and history. Certainly teach your daughter about the pill, but do not expect today's high school teachers to tell her when to swallow it.

Teaching values in a formal, organized way is in the same category as philosophy. It is too early. The student needs multiple concretes first. He has to experience life, supplemented by what he learns from literature and history. The only real way to teach values in the early years is through the way the whole education system is organized. Objectivist education blends perfectly with the Objectivist code of values. The essence of Objectivist education is training minds. That does consist of teaching values because, according to Objectivism, the primary value is the mind. Every time you give a child the proper motivation and tell him, "This is going to enhance your understanding," every time you teach him structure or integration or the proper method, you are teaching him the value of thinking and logic. Every time you give him a proper conceptual subject and expand his understanding, you are upholding for him, in concrete form, the paramount value of thought. If you do this properly, you do not have to give him special lectures on values. By the time he gets to *Atlas Shrugged*, it will be self-evident to him. If you properly teach history, literature, mathematics, and science, the child will absorb the values of independence, individuality, and self-esteem as logical consequences of thought.

The final concrete-oriented way to inculcate values, beyond the curricular subject matter is by the practical daily requirements—the actual rules of living—that the child must obey at school. He gets his value orientation partly from his own observations and the subjects you are teaching him and partly by simply living and finding out what his life requires of him. School is profoundly important to these young children. The rules that you institute are very significant in teaching children certain values. Although this is an example from a college context, a letter I received from a student will illustrate what I mean:

> My first year at the University of California at Berkeley, I went to the Dean of Students to discuss a problem with the food at the dormitories. He asked what group I represented. When I said that I represented only myself, he said that he was not interested in individual views, and that he would hear me out only if I represented a group. I protested that my views were as important as those of any group and he countered that I could starve to death if I didn't like the food and told me to leave. The message was a clear preview of my entire education at Berkeley. The individual never counted

there, only the group, which seemed to have an identity and
life of its own.

If you have years of that kind of collectivism, not taught necessarily but just a requirement of existence—you cannot move without
the group, you cannot lift blocks without the group, you cannot disagree without the group—you are certainly going to turn out collec-
tivists who share collectivist values.

By the same token, if you have rational living conditions, you
will turn out rational individualists. That is a very powerful adjunct
to a proper curriculum. In order to teach rational living, every procedure in the school has to be calculated and not simply established by
tradition or pragmatic decisions of the moment. Every single aspect
has to be planned: the grading procedure; what the child does if there
is an injustice; what demands he can make; what to do if he does
not want to play with the other children; how you treat absenteeism;
what you do about discipline. All procedures and policies have to
be developed so that a proper attitude toward himself, his powers,
and other students is inculcated. The life's work of the owner of the
school is to determine how to organize and accomplish this.

CHAPTER FOUR

Teacher Skills

Now that we know the general purpose, the methods, and the curriculum of a proper education, our final task is to determine the skills required by those whose vocation it is to implement them.

1. What specific techniques should teachers employ to achieve the goals, the methods, and the curriculum so far discussed?

2. What is necessary to train teachers who can successfully deliver the proper curriculum?

3. Under what political system can we hope to get these teachers and why don't we have them today?

The Lecture Method versus the Discussion Method

The two main rivals for delivering the thinking methods and subjects that are to be taught are the lecture method and the discussion method.

Lecturing means continual talking by the teacher to the students, delivering material that is prepared in advance. The students essentially listen, take notes, and perhaps occasionally ask a question, but that is a peripheral phenomenon. The discussion method is predominantly talking by the students. The teacher, in some sense, guides the discussion. He may have a lesson plan, he may try to elicit specific material from the class, or he may ask pointed questions and do whatever he can to maneuver the discussion in a certain direction. But the basic distinction between these two methods is that the class is essentially silent during the lecture method while it is the dominant voice during the discussion method.

When I went to school in Canada, we had organized lectures starting in kindergarten. The only time we had discussion, everybody moaned and groaned because it meant the teacher had not prepared and was killing the period. In contrast, when I came to the United States, it was rare to find a lecture even in a college class. An objective survey of the advantages and disadvantages claimed for each method should allow you to adjudicate the merits of these two techniques.

The single essential virtue of lecturing is: the flow of material is controlled by a knowledgeable mind trained in the field. Ignorant novices (the class) do not determine the flow of the material. The teacher knows what motivation is necessary and builds it right into his lecture. He stays just long enough to establish it and then moves on. He knows what information is essential and what is peripheral, irrelevant, or overcomplicated. He decides it in advance and does not waste time or focus. He does not introduce needless confusion. He suppresses whole irrelevant bodies of data or useless extraneous blind alleys. He gives the stripped-down essentials. He decides what integrations should be made, when a concept needs to be broken down to its percepts, and how to order the material logically.

A class discussion unavoidably is burdened with irrelevancies. You cannot blame the students who do not know the subject. If they knew what was relevant, they would not need the material. The class discussion—however well controlled—is governed to a significant extent by random private associations out of any logical order. The students will jump too fast to a point or take forever and go too slow. They will be too concrete-bound or they will be too floating (detached from reality).

All of those crucial questions of presentation, which affect the ability to grasp the subject and the ability to grasp thinking methods, have to be decided either by someone who knows the subject or by those who do not. And that is the essential difference between the two methods.

To engage in group discussion with a group who knows nothing about the subject is pointless. It leads to incredible boredom for the best students and a tremendous amount of wasted time spent on irrelevancies without regard for logical order. The discussion advocates (who outnumber lecturing advocates about a thousand to one) are scandalized by such statements. "We do not just have a random bull session. The teacher has to guide the discussion; he has to elicit relevant points. He is the orchestra leader and the class is the band."

The only real hope of success in this guided method is if you are lucky enough to have a passive class—one that, in effect, is comprised of puppets with you pulling the strings. That really amounts to abandoning the discussion method. The class, in such a context, is not really initiating and following their own lead; they basically answer yes or no, while you force leading questions down their throat. That is not a real discussion; that is a sham.

To illustrate: if the teacher says, "Columbus discovered America in 1492," that is rejected as dogmatic and authoritarian lecturing. If the teacher says, "What do you think, Miss Smith? Did he discover it in 1492 or not?" And when Miss Smith replies, "Well, I feel he did," that is considered discussion. Obviously, there is no advantage in that procedure.

Another objection to lecturing that is raised is: If lecturing by an expert is the right method, why do we even need his physical presence? He could just write a book, lay the whole thing out with the right examples and the right integrations, point-by-point, and grade the level of difficulty according to the abilities of the students. All that teaching need consist of is a fabulous library and a librarian. The student comes in, is given a reading list and reads the various books in order, maybe with a question period every few months. There are people who do recommend this. They think that the live teacher is completely dispensable and that education should be a student browsing through a properly organized library. This is neither a valid objection nor an effective method of education in the early years. When a student reaches fifteen and has a certain basic grounding, he may be ready for such a procedure but not in the early years. Certainly, reading is an invaluable supplement to education, but it is very much harder to learn from a book than from a good lecture.

Of course, if the teacher merely rattles off prepared material (which would be the same as just reading aloud), then a book could be even better because at least you could stop in a book and review. That is not my idea of a proper lecture. A good lecturer, even though his material is completely prepared in advance, does not simply deliver it. He constantly monitors his audience. He gets clues from them at every moment, as to what they understand and what they do not understand, what they care about and what they do not care about, and he adapts his presentation on the spot to their requirements. He adapts the form of his delivery to the moment-by-moment requirements of the actual students in front of him. No book can do this.

For example, suppose you are lecturing from prepared material and you see expressions of widespread bafflement, or a frown that you did not expect, or a murmur of surprise. You immediately think, "I have to stop. Something is not getting through." Maybe you have to slow down and repeat, maybe you need to restate, maybe you need to further explain extemporaneously until the frown disappears.

Other times you might feel a sudden pocket of boredom in the room. The audience attention falls; you start to see yawns. You get the vibrations of "We already know this," so you speed up; you drop out segments of your prepared material and forge ahead. If you think the context warrants it, you may stop when you realize the students are not really as motivated as you thought they were. If you ask them why they are bored, they will always tell you because children are very blunt about that. You throw in a joke, liven it up, and get them back on the track.

A lecturer has countless tools at his command to ease the flow of material into specific minds. He has tempo, emphasis, voice quality, gestures, pauses, volume, and so forth. In other words, a lecturer not only can tailor his material to a specific audience, he can also make it an exercise in drama, color, urgency, and emotional excitement. He can both inform and move his listeners. And, of course, everyone learns much better if reason and emotion are united. It is virtually impossible for a textbook to do this, unless written by a genius, and I cannot imagine what motive a genius would have to write a textbook.

Good lecturing can make a class an experience in theater, adapted to the unique students present at the moment. A book is aimed at a universal audience, any abstract rational mind. A lecturer is much more concretely oriented. This is why I think neither books nor audio/video/computer technology will replace teachers: they cannot monitor and adapt to give exactly what is required precisely when it is required. A child can be reading a book and suddenly be baffled by something in the text, and that one moment of bafflement will wipe out all intelligibility, whereas a good teacher will see that frown, dissect it, and dispel it before going any further.

One argument against the lecture method is that it makes students too passive: they do not learn to think; they just absorb. We learn to think by the lecturer's presentation and the methods that he stresses in presenting the material. Nobody learns to think by talking aloud when he is ignorant. If you are ignorant, you learn primarily by listening (a much-maligned word in education today) to a properly organized presentation. There is certainly a value in speaking, even if you are ignorant. It gives you a chance to marshal your thoughts, organize your ideas, and grope for formulations. But this type of verbalizing on your own is much more effectively done in writing at home where you have unlimited time and no pressure to perform or show off, and where your chaos and confusion does not waste everybody else's time. It is not a valid objection that the educational methods that I advocate inculcate passivity—not if conjoined with massive doses of writing at home, which are then analyzed on an individual basis by the teacher.

There is a more valid objection to pure lecturing: a lecturer, even one who monitors carefully, has a very limited insight into the student's mind. It is only what he can glean from external evidence. If I see eyes glaze over or hear a lot of shuffling and coughing, I know something is wrong, but I cannot get inside another's consciousness. Sometimes the external evidence can be grossly misleading. Every teacher has had the experience of students sitting in the front, nodding at all the right points, giving you every indication that they are motivated and understand the lecture. But when you read their exams, it is obvious that they have no clue about the material. They just learned to nod like Pavlov's dog. My argument is that if you really want to check on what students know, you have to probe. You have to question them. You have to let them talk. The more they talk, the more you find out, and thus we are plunged back into the discussion method.

The discussion method has the advantage over the lecturing method of revealing a student's consciousness to the teacher. Their questions and comments unmistakably reveal their motivation, their interests, their understanding, their errors, and their confusions, giving you that information in a way that simply observing them cannot do.

Nevertheless, the fatal flaw is that, however well guided, discussion has an inherent tendency to become chaos: subject-switching, arbitrary assertions, concrete-bound. That is because the initiative is being taken by the ignorant. The result of such discussions is that the class comes to the conclusion that knowledge is simply a process of boring, endless talk, that it is all subjective, that nobody knows anything. Ten years of class discussion is a recipe for training skeptics. You would have to be the most unusual genius to emerge from that kind of schooling as anything else.

It is true that some discussion leaders are better than others. There are brilliant discussion leaders who can take the most far-out question, field it so the student feels that he has been answered and get right back on the track. They can dominate the process so that they minimize the damage. But that is the most they can do—minimize the damage; they cannot eliminate it. So I am not an advocate of what is called the "Socratic method," for general education in the primary or secondary schools, or even at the undergraduate level. I do think the Socratic method or the tutorial is valuable in certain contexts for advanced students. I have used it myself, but it presupposes that the student has a wealth of knowledge. He has a foundation for his comments, explorations, and questions. I do not think it works successfully in a large group because even two people will have divergent directions in which they want to go. If you have too many different perspectives, the exercise just sprawls into meaningless verbiage. I have found it very beneficial to give a few bright students an advanced tutorial because, when they have the proper foundation, it is essential for them to discuss and question in the standard discussion method. But to comparative beginners, it is a waste of time. They are too ignorant to discuss meaningfully.

The actual reason for the prevalence of the discussion method has nothing to do with Socrates. Discussion is the method of skeptics and subjectivists. It reflects the idea of the group above reality, which is today's dominant educational philosophy, thanks to Dewey.

In evaluating this issue, we find another false alternative, as we do almost everywhere in education. In a pure lecture, the class is completely silent. The teacher is concerned simply to deliver the material, and takes limited cognizance of the consciousness of the students. He gives the data and hopes that it enters and takes root.

The discussion method, on the other hand, is very concerned with self-expression—with consciousness expressing itself—but does not recognize the need for any knowledge of reality for that purpose. This is the same basic dichotomy of the intrinsic versus the subjective. The pure lecturer typically organizes his data and wants to pour it in the student's mind which is more or less viewed as a passive receptacle. The pure discusser wants the minds of the students to guide the process, apart from the data of reality. Again, here as elsewhere, objectivity should be the guiding solution; the proper union of existence and consciousness—of data and the student's awareness.

The resolution to this dichotomy is what I call "lecturing in chunks." First of all, the teacher or communicator does have a full lecture prepared. He decides in advance, from his knowledge of the field and his audience, what motivation to supply, what context to count on, what material is essential and what structure to follow. He knows when to generalize, when to concretize, and what examples are the best. He has all the advantages of the lecture, and he delivers it just as he has prepared it.

The difference is that it is punctuated now and again by intervals of controlled class discussion. The timing of these intervals is not decided by the students. They are decided in advance by the lecturer, as the material permits. The teacher has to divide the total lecture into units which are relatively self-contained and are logical stopping points, like a book is divided into chapters. The lecture is, in effect, carved up into three or four different issues which are determined by the original structure, the three or four self-contained points. Each point should be such that you have to grasp it in total before there is any interruption. It has to be developed as a whole: the beginning, the middle, the end. Until the class gets that point, it does not have enough knowledge to start asking questions or making comments. Each chunk is like an atom: an indivisible amount of the lecture. If you break that atom, the student loses the point.

During the development of one chunk, I permit no interruptions. It has to be perfectly structured and every element is needed so you cannot let the class interfere. If they bring in the wrong question or the wrong observation at the wrong time, they can wipe out the preceding material and just confuse everybody. There is a point where it is too early to let your students ask a question, even too early to let them say that they are unclear. I first discovered this from Ayn Rand. I was brought up with the idea that if ever you are unclear about any point, you should stop the teacher right there and say that you do not get it. When I would tell Miss Rand that I did not understand a point while she was answering my questions, she would often reply, "Well, of course you don't understand; you didn't let me finish." I was baffled by that until I finally grasped that integration as a total can occur which makes any given unit within it clear. If you ask certain questions at the wrong time, you make learning impossible. If you keep quiet and even learn to endure momentarily the fact that you do not get something, often a few minutes later you retroactively get it.

In these chunks, I do not allow interruptions even though the students may be confused or not interested. Reality, in these moments, sets the terms. You must say to the students, in effect, "Right now, you be quiet and listen. I know better than you what you need to hear at this moment." This is where the idea that children should be seen and not heard has a valid application. Once the unit has been presented, some controlled discussion is valuable. It is impossible to say what the ratio of discussion to material should be, because it depends on many factors, such as the quality of the discussion, what the next chunk is, how much time you have for the total syllabus, and the level of student confusion. As a rough average, I try to make it three or four minutes of lecturing to one minute of discussion. In an hour class, I would aim for ten to fifteen minutes of discussion, other things being equal. By "discussion," I do not mean you sit back and say, "OK, your turn now." I mean a very controlled, delimited discussion for four purposes only:

1. To assess motivation
2. To evaluate understanding

3. To allow exploration

4. To provide a respite

- **Motivation:** You have to gauge the students' motivation and supplement it if necessary. If you see they are not too interested, you have to find out why right away. Let them tell you why they are not interested and have them make the best case they can, as to why this material is not worth knowing. Count on the fact that you can refute their argument.

- **Cognition:** You must check whether or not the students are grasping the material. Is there a need for clarification? Are there any errors you can see running through their comments? Are there any points that need review? Now is the time for it.

- **Exploration:** I do allow a bit of freewheeling. Let students jump all over the map because, within limits, it has the value of giving them a glimmer of the connections between this unit and the rest of what they are doing. What further questions are there? What further applications? Where else does this subject go? It gives them a chance to grope for their own conclusions.

- **R&R:** I do not believe that people (and certainly not children) can focus optimally hour after hour after hour. After ten minutes of pressure buildup where you are exhorting their faculty of focus, a little while to let off steam is appropriate. Let's face it; it does not really make much difference if they pay attention to what the other students are saying. In fact, it may be preferable that they don't.

Again, the amounts of time given to these periods are variable. It depends on the class, the subject, and the circumstances. This concession to the discussion approach is given with the condition that discussion is only an adjunct to the lecture method. The discussion functions as a supplement to what a good lecturer does anyway: observe the audience and adapt. It permits you, though, a deeper penetration into the students' minds. Lecturing is still the primary; the discussion is merely a perfecting of what you are accomplishing by the lecture method. That is why I regard myself as essentially in the lecturing camp.

In conclusion of this point, if you are going to practice this, I want to warn you that it is very tricky to keep the right balance, to not let the discussion swamp the lecture. You have to keep the momentum of your ideas and your presentation going. You will get many weird comments out of left field because that is where the kids are when they do not know the material. Some students will be threatened by what you say. There is always somebody who takes personally something you say and is outraged. There are frightened students who do not dare speak, and you want to try to get them involved. And you have to do all this while moving fast enough not to bore the bright ones, and slow enough not to lose the less capable ones. This does assume that the students are grouped by ability as far as it is feasible, always keeping in mind that even in a group of three there will be a high-average-low split. The class would be roughly based on age, with accessory classes for the very fast and slow. Administratively, this method of teaching is cheaper and more practical. Because it is completely controlled by the teacher, it does not require small classes—a modern superficiality. This teaching method is a very skilled technique, although not one learned in college. It is what I regard as the objective technique, as opposed to the intrinsic or the subjective.

Training Teachers

My view of teacher training institutions is dealt with in my lecture "Why Johnny Can't Think."

To decide whether a teachers college has a legitimate function or not, you have to ask: What skills does teaching require that can be reduced to a body of knowledge and be taught through courses? Teaching obviously requires many things that cannot be taught in an educational institution. For instance, it requires motivation. You must have the desire to teach. But a school of education does not give you motivation; it presupposes it. Teaching requires common sense, it requires experience, and it requires knowledge of the subject matter. None of these comes from a professional school of education.

Let's review some plausible candidates for subjects that could be taught through courses at a teachers college.

Psychology. Good teaching does not require a knowledge of psychology. There have been many brilliant teachers who know zero about the cure for neurosis, the dynamics of psychosexual development, the needs of the unconscious, the causes of homosexuality, or the problems of self-esteem. By the same token, there are many psychologists who know or claim to know all of these things inside out and yet are hopeless teachers. There is no relationship at all between knowledge of psychology and ability to teach. There are only two things from psychology that a teacher has to know: that humans have to be motivated in order to learn and that they can only understand what is logical. Obviously, you do not require a course in psychology to grasp these two points. I do not make these comments because of some kind of anti-psychological bias on my part. I have the greatest respect for psychology. If you are a therapist concerned with the subconscious, you are trying to change it or probe its contents.

But teaching is not concerned with the subconscious; it is aimed at consciousness, at the intellect. It is concerned with the communication of knowledge and intellectual methods. If the potential student is so sick mentally that you cannot address his consciousness as such, then he is unteachable. He is outside the domain of the teacher and of education, and it is a complete corruption and confusion of function to mix those two.

Here is a perfect analogy stolen from the Greeks. To coach football, you assume a healthy body and teach specific conscious motions. If the player is too sick physically, such as with a broken leg, you send him to a hospital or to a specialist to get him to the condition where he can benefit from your football instruction. The same applies here. In teaching, you must assume a mind that is capable of functioning. If not, get the child out of the class and into a hospital or therapy or a home that will be of benefit to him. I think that so-called educational psychologists today are literally destroying teaching by trying to turn teachers into amateur psychologists who are concerned with the subconscious of their charges while ignoring their minds. You no longer bother whether Johnny got a D or an A in French; you try to find out whether he has an inverted Oedipal regression or not. That is what is put on the report card and that is what the teacher is focused on. I regard that as incredibly vicious and destructive. Psychology is very valuable in its place, but it is harmful if it is not kept in its place. Educational psychology does more harm than any other aspect of teacher training.

Methodology. Methodology as taught today in teachers colleges means arbitrary trivia formalized into useless systems. For instance, there is a methodology of being a janitor. There is a methodology of teaching janitorial science and analyzing the concepts that are involved in teaching janitors.

There is only one basic methodology that has to be known by a good teacher and that is the method of thinking: how to be logical, how to hold a context, how to respect the hierarchy of knowledge, how to abstract and integrate. Without question, you need this kind of method in order to teach. But the point is, you need it to do anything at all. It is not a need distinctive to teaching and it is not the preserve of some special school for teachers.

Thinking has to be learned in grade school as part of becoming educated. That is the whole purpose of education, as we have seen. A proper education is a decade-long training in how to think—in the conditions, the processes, and the methods of thought. If you do not get it from years of a proper general education, and/or from your experience of life by the time you reach adulthood, you are not going to get it from a special graduate school for teachers. I want to make this one qualification. I can see the value of a few books and even a few courses for a potential teacher, primarily giving him tips on how to apply the thinking methods he already knows to the teaching situation. But there is not that much to say on this topic. What is essential is epistemology—a knowledge of objectivity, integration, context, hierarchy—which people should receive in regular education. Education is a far different field than medicine or law where there is a vast specialized knowledge. Teaching is not comparable to these fields. It is not a complex specialized subject, in that way. In fact, you do not even have to know epistemology as such. It is possible to be able to think clearly, assuming you have a decent education, without knowing the formal theory of thinking.

What a good teacher requires aside from thinking ability and knowledge of his subject is enthusiasm for his subject and the desire to make it known. Thereafter, what he needs is experience and intelligent reflection. I say close down the schools of education. At most, all that is required is a one-year post-high school course on practical advice: tips on motivating; how to give exams with the least pain; managing discipline problems; how to organize your curriculum—but certainly not years of study.

The Politics of Education

Our schools today are terrible, both philosophically and politically. Why don't we have the kind of education that we should? It is possible to find a good school today but it is an exception on the periphery created by people who can circumvent the double taxation, the compulsory schooling laws, the teachers' unions, and the bureaucratic requirements. A certain kind of social system is necessary to have the caliber of teachers who can provide the appropriate education. Compulsory education is incompatible, in the long run, with that type of education.

What kind of society provides a good education? The answer lies in Ayn Rand's principle that reason and freedom are corollaries. If reason rules men philosophically, if reason is what they respect and exercise, then they will naturally insist on leaving men free to think and act accordingly, and we will end up with an individualistic, free, capitalistic society. Once men are free, the best among them in all fields will rise to the top, including in the field of education. The people most committed to thought and conceptual training will ultimately set the terms. Practically speaking, they will demonstrate their value in the marketplace. There will not be a state monopoly of education; there will be competing schools. The better the educators, the more their students will get the good jobs, achieve success, make money, and live a happy life. The anti-conceptual schools will turn out perceivable failures and will simply lose out in the marketplace. This is plain capitalism. The better mousetrap will win out in the end, if men are free. In education, "better" means conceptual. People at all levels are dissatisfied with what is going on in education today, even though they have no idea why. They flock to schools like Montessori because they can see that they at least achieve something.

There is a deeper reason why a conceptual education will be the ultimate product of a free society. Reason is the motivating premise of a free society, to begin with. Reason leads to freedom, politically. This is what men are imbued with, and therefore, this is what they are going to teach their youngsters. Reason means the exercise of the conceptual faculty. In other words, the same basic premise that leads to freedom will lead to a pro-reason, pro-conceptual education.

Just as reason and freedom are corollaries, so too are faith and force. If men reject reason, they have no way to deal with one another or resolve disputes except, ultimately, by coercion. You have to use force where reason is abandoned. The final expression of that is going to be some kind of institutionalized force by the government. Once you have that, then obedience and conformity rise to the top. The whole system rests on the idea that the individual should efface himself, keep quiet, and obey the leader. Unavoidably, you have an anti-mind atmosphere.

Today, practically speaking, the best educators are throttled because of the state monopoly. Mediocrity is entrenched in the field. You have the socialization of education. It works exactly like the post office, for exactly the same reason. There is no competition possible: it is a direct invitation to stagnation, mediocrity, and complete indifference to the actual function of the institution. A mind outside the system has no chance to compete or even to get a foot inside the system. We are approaching that now, as evidenced by the difficulty of getting a teaching job in the humanities if you do not subscribe to today's orthodoxy and the impossibility of teaching if you do not belong to the union.

The deeper cause, of course, as to why you are going to end up with an anti-conceptual education in a statist society, is because the basic philosophy which led to statism will emerge in education as well. An active antipathy to the mind was the root that led people to the all-powerful state. That is its motivating premise, and that is certainly going to show up in the schools in every possible way. In the United States today that antipathy to reason is the Kantian philosophy. Reality is unknowable, truth is what the collective decrees, and the most important thing is conformity. You can see that education in the United States subscribes wholeheartedly to this underlying philosophic premise, the very premise that led us to a collectivist society.

We not only have generalized adulation of the group (group schooling), we have now reached the unprecedented and abysmal depths of having pressure-group schooling. We have female studies classes, black classes, Chicano classes, and bilingual classes. We have the utter collapse of objectivity and principles in the curriculum in favor of Balkanized feuding groups, each trying to seize the student and inject their propaganda. They proclaim proudly how subjective they are. Their concern is to give the students their version, and their version is always and only the concretes of their particular heritage and alleged achievements.

Ethically, the philosophy of unreason and statism embraces altruism. Altruism leads in the end to egalitarianism, which is defined as the belief in the equality of all men before the law. This is not the meaning that altruists ascribe to the term. Egalitarianism, for them, is the hatred of the good for being the good, and the reward of the incompetent for being incompetent. This, too, has reached its climax in education in countless shocking ways. An obvious example is the collapse of entrance requirements. It is considered immoral for a student to have to know something in order to pass from grade two to grade three, that he has just as much right to be in grade three as anybody else, or to be a brain surgeon, or to do anything. Demanding knowledge is unfair because it violates equality.

However, the worst horror of egalitarianism in education is the "mainstreaming of the handicapped." We mean here, not just the physically, but the mentally handicapped as mandated by federal law. Up to ten times more per handicapped student is spent than what is required for a regular student. It is a requirement that he not be treated in separate schools suited to his particular mental handicap. By federal law these children who, through no fault of their own, are in a completely different dimension must be placed in regular classes. Otherwise, the schools do not receive federal subsidies. Try and imagine conducting a class in which it is mandated that the mentally handicapped be an integral part of the instructional process. In the name of egalitarianism, why should the fact that the child is mindless or retarded deprive him of science and mathematics? This is the deliberate, willful sacrifice of the mind to the so-called need of the mindless.

Educators today claim that their plight is the problem of achieving both excellence and equity but since we cannot have both, a choice has to be made. If we have standards in education, we are immoral because we are depriving those who cannot live up to the standards of an equal education. If we collapse all education to the lowest common denominator, everybody gets an education lacking both substance and value. This has become one of the thorniest problems of education: the conundrum of "quality versus equality."

This is a dilemma no philosophy is going to solve. You absolutely do have to choose between quality and equality, given their definitions. It *is* "either-or." The particular choice that today's educators are making follows unavoidably from their ethics, which itself follows from their anti-reason. The first thing to be dispensed with in this kind of egalitarian atmosphere is a conceptual approach to education. A conceptual approach takes tremendous work, commitment, and dedication. It does not happen automatically. If you leave men to what happens automatically, they have recourse only to their perceptual functions. If educators ignore conceptual training, all that will come to replace it will be exactly what we have today: a hodgepodge of perceptual concretes and blind memory, in no order, with no message. If you see this overall picture—from politics back to ethics back to epistemology—you see that it all leads unavoidably to the collapse of education. It is a straight line from *The Critique of Pure Reason* to Johnny who can't think—a straight, tragic line.

Is this a chicken-and-egg situation? You need the right government to get better schools, which are made virtually impossible with all of today's restrictions. Yet you need better schools to get a better government or where are the properly educated politicians going to come from? Which comes first: better politicians or better school teachers? The answer is neither. Both of these are effects. If they come at all, they are going to come together. What has to come first is their root and that is philosophy. Ayn Rand once offered the observation that it is philosophy that got us into this state and it is only philosophy that is going to get us out of it.

First, you have to launch a purely philosophical campaign aimed at a small, dedicated nucleus of intellectuals who go to the core of a society's irrationalism and fight for a renaissance of reason. When you get a foothold in the universities, you make forays in both directions at once, in the direction of better government and of better schools. The hope is that you will start a virtuous circle and each will help the other.

If the philosophy departments lay the groundwork, gradually we can hope there will be better political candidates and better school teachers emerging. In a continuing symbiotic relationship, these better candidates will make the schools gradually freer while these better teachers will make each decade's politicians a bit more rational.

That is what I am proposing with *Teaching Johnny to Think*, using Objectivism as the base. It is a long, bleak process at times, but I do think that there is a chance of succeeding. Simply the act of parents and teachers seeking information to improve their children's education gives hope to the idea that the battle for a proper education is winnable. As parents and educators, your role is to present a reasoned argument for the implementation of methods, curricula, and structure that will develop the full potential of our future generations. You must enlist sympathetic politicians and like-minded individuals to promote an objective, cognitive education for your children's success—and the country's survival.

Made in the USA
San Bernardino, CA
10 July 2014